Olfactory Ethics

The Politics Of Smell

By Riha Hazina

Introduction

Introduction

We live in a world saturated with smells. From the moment we wake to the aroma of coffee or the crisp morning air, to the lingering scent of dinner as we drift to sleep, our olfactory sense is constantly engaged, shaping our experiences, memories, and emotions. Yet, despite its pervasive influence, smell often remains a silent, unacknowledged partner in our daily lives. We talk about what we see, hear, taste, and touch, but rarely do we delve into the complexities of our olfactory experiences. This book aims to break that silence, to bring the often-overlooked sense of smell into the forefront of our ethical considerations.

"Olfactory Ethics: The Politics of Smell" explores the intricate and often hidden ways in which smell intersects with power, social justice, identity, and our understanding of the world around us. It delves into the ethical dimensions of our relationship with smell, examining how our olfactory perceptions are shaped by cultural norms, social hierarchies, and political agendas.

The book challenges us to consider the ethical implications of a world where smells are increasingly manipulated, controlled, and commodified. It examines how the fragrance industry influences our olfactory preferences, how smells are used to create and reinforce social divisions, and how the right to breathe clean air is often unequally distributed. We will explore the use of smell in surveillance and security, the stigma associated with certain smells and diseases, and the ways in which olfactory experiences can be used to evoke memories, shape identities, and even influence our political choices.

"Olfactory Ethics" is not simply about pleasant or unpleasant smells. It's about recognizing that our olfactory sense is deeply intertwined with our social, political, and ethical lives. It's about understanding how our sense of smell can be used to manipulate, control, and discriminate, but also how it can be a source of pleasure, connection, and understanding. This book invites you to embark on a journey into the fascinating and complex world of

5

smell, to question your own olfactory assumptions, and to consider the ethical responsibilities that come with inhabiting a world of scents.

Chapter One: The Nose Knows: An Introduction to Olfactory Ethics

Our sense of smell, often relegated to the background of our conscious experience, plays a far more profound role in shaping our lives than we might realize. It's a primal sense, deeply rooted in our evolutionary history, intimately linked to our emotions, memories, and even our survival instincts. This chapter serves as a foundational exploration of olfaction, introducing the basic mechanisms of how we smell, the unique power of scent in shaping our perceptions and behaviors, and laying the groundwork for understanding the complex ethical considerations that arise from our engagement with the olfactory world.

The Biological Basis of Smell:

The journey of a smell begins with volatile molecules, tiny airborne particles released from various sources – a blooming flower, a freshly baked loaf of bread, a passing car's exhaust. These molecules travel through the air and enter our nasal passages, where they encounter the olfactory epithelium, a postage stamp-sized patch of tissue located high in the nasal cavity. Within this epithelium lie millions of olfactory receptor neurons, specialized cells equipped with tiny hair-like projections called cilia. These cilia are coated with olfactory receptors, proteins that act as molecular locks, each designed to bind with specific odorant molecules, like a key fitting into its designated lock.

When an odorant molecule binds to its corresponding receptor, it triggers a cascade of biochemical events within the olfactory neuron, ultimately generating an electrical signal. This signal travels along the neuron's axon, which bundles together with other axons to form the olfactory nerve. The olfactory nerve carries these signals directly to the olfactory bulb, a structure located at the base of the brain, just above the nasal cavity.

The olfactory bulb acts as a relay station, sorting and processing the incoming olfactory signals. From the olfactory bulb, information is transmitted to various regions of the brain, including the amygdala, the hippocampus, and the orbitofrontal cortex. The amygdala is involved in processing emotions, particularly fear and pleasure, which explains why certain smells can evoke strong emotional responses. The hippocampus plays a crucial role in memory formation, linking smells to specific events and experiences. The orbitofrontal cortex is involved in decision-making and assigning value to sensory experiences, influencing our preferences for certain smells over others.

The Unique Power of Scent:

Unlike our other senses, which are routed through the thalamus, a sensory relay center in the brain, before reaching the cortex, smell has a direct pathway to areas involved in emotion and memory. This direct connection explains the powerful and often immediate impact that smells can have on our emotional state and our ability to recall past experiences. A whiff of perfume might instantly transport us back to a childhood memory, the aroma of a particular spice might trigger a wave of nostalgia for a distant place, or the smell of smoke might evoke a primal fear response.

The intimate link between smell and emotion is also evident in the phenomenon of olfactory-evoked autobiographical memories, also known as "Proustian memories," named after the French novelist Marcel Proust, who famously described how the taste and smell of a madeleine cake triggered a vivid recollection of his childhood. These olfactory-triggered memories are often more intense and emotionally charged than memories evoked by other senses.

Furthermore, smell plays a significant role in our social interactions, even if we are not always consciously aware of it. Pheromones, chemical signals released by individuals, can influence the behavior and physiology of others within the same species. While the role of pheromones in human behavior is still debated, there is evidence that they can influence mate selection, menstrual synchrony, and even maternal bonding. Our body odor, a complex mixture of volatile organic compounds, can also convey information about our health, age, and even our emotional state.

The Dawn of Olfactory Ethics:

The profound influence of smell on our perceptions, emotions, behaviors, and social interactions raises a host of ethical questions that have largely been neglected until recently. As our understanding of the olfactory system deepens, and as technologies emerge that allow us to manipulate and control smells in unprecedented ways, the need for a robust ethical framework to guide our engagement with the olfactory world becomes increasingly apparent.

Olfactory ethics, as an emerging field of inquiry, seeks to address these ethical challenges by exploring questions such as:

- How can we ensure that the right to breathe clean air is protected for all individuals, regardless of their socioeconomic status or geographical location?

- What are the ethical implications of using smells to manipulate consumer behavior or to create and reinforce social divisions?

- How can we balance the use of smell in security and surveillance with the need to protect individual privacy and autonomy?

- What are the ethical responsibilities of the fragrance industry in ensuring the safety and well-being of consumers and the environment?

- How can we promote olfactory literacy and encourage a more nuanced and ethical engagement with the smellscape?

These are just a few of the many questions that olfactory ethics seeks to address. As we navigate an increasingly complex and odor-saturated world, the need to understand the ethical dimensions of our relationship with smell will only become more pressing. This book serves as an invitation to delve deeper into this fascinating and often overlooked realm of ethical inquiry, to explore the intricate connections between smell, power, social justice, and our shared humanity.

Chapter Two: The Politics of Scent: Power, Control, and the Olfactory

Smell, often considered a passive sense, is deeply entwined with power dynamics and social control. Throughout history, the ability to manipulate and control smells has been wielded by those in power to shape public perception, reinforce social hierarchies, and maintain order. This chapter explores the intricate relationship between smell and politics, examining how scent has been used as a tool of oppression and resistance, a marker of social status and identity, and a means of shaping the environment to reflect dominant ideologies.

The Olfactory Landscape of Power:

In many ancient societies, the use of incense and perfumes was closely associated with religious and political authority. Incense was burned in temples and palaces to appease deities, create a sacred atmosphere, and elevate the status of rulers. The Egyptians, for example, used elaborate incense rituals in their religious ceremonies, believing that the fragrant smoke carried prayers and offerings to the gods. Similarly, in ancient Rome, emperors were often depicted holding incense burners, symbolizing their divine right to rule.

The association of pleasant smells with power and purity extended beyond religious contexts. In medieval Europe, the use of perfumes and spices was a privilege enjoyed primarily by the wealthy elite. Strong perfumes were used to mask the unpleasant odors of unsanitary living conditions, while spices were imported from distant lands at great expense, serving as a symbol of wealth and status. The lower classes, on the other hand, were often associated with the stench of poverty and manual labor.

This olfactory hierarchy reflected and reinforced the existing social order. Pleasant smells were associated with the ruling class, creating an aura of divinity, superiority, and refinement.

Unpleasant smells, on the other hand, were used to stigmatize and marginalize the poor and marginalized. This association of smell with social status persists in many societies today, albeit in more subtle forms.

Olfactory Control and Social Order:

The manipulation of smell has also been used as a tool of social control. In the 18th and 19th centuries, during the rise of industrialization and urbanization, the stench of overcrowded cities became a major concern for public health officials. The miasma theory, which held that diseases were caused by bad air, led to efforts to control and eliminate unpleasant odors in urban environments. Sewage systems were built, streets were cleaned, and public spaces were disinfected with strong-smelling chemicals.

While these efforts were aimed at improving public health, they also served to control and regulate the behavior of the urban poor. The association of poverty with unpleasant smells led to the implementation of sanitation policies that often targeted the living conditions of the lower classes. These policies, while ostensibly aimed at eliminating disease, also served to reinforce social hierarchies and maintain order in a rapidly changing urban landscape.

Smell as a Weapon of Oppression:

The manipulation of smell has also been used as a weapon of oppression and violence. During the Holocaust, the Nazis used Zyklon B, a highly toxic pesticide with a distinct almond-like odor, to murder millions of Jews in gas chambers. The smell of Zyklon B became a symbol of terror and death, forever etched in the memories of survivors.

In more recent times, malodorants, chemicals that produce highly unpleasant smells, have been used as a form of crowd control and torture. "Skunk bombs," for example, which emit a foul-smelling liquid, have been used by law enforcement agencies to disperse protesters and control unruly crowds. The use of malodorants in these contexts raises serious ethical concerns about the potential for psychological harm and the violation of human rights.

Olfactory Resistance and Subversion:

While smell has been used as a tool of power and control, it has also been used as a form of resistance and subversion. In the antebellum South, enslaved Africans used strong-smelling herbs and spices to mask their scent from slave catchers and to create a sense of community and cultural identity. The use of these smells was a way of asserting agency and resisting the dehumanizing conditions of slavery.

In more recent times, activists have used smell as a form of protest and social commentary. In 2011, during the Occupy Wall Street movement, protesters used strong-smelling substances like vinegar and garlic to disrupt police attempts to clear their encampments. The use of smell in these contexts highlights the potential for olfactory activism to challenge power structures and raise awareness of social injustices.

The Olfactory Construction of Identity:

Smell plays a crucial role in the construction of individual and collective identities. Our personal scent, a unique blend of body odor, perfumes, and environmental factors, can communicate information about our gender, age, ethnicity, and social status. Cultural norms and expectations also shape our perceptions of what smells are considered acceptable or desirable.

The fragrance industry, a multi-billion dollar global enterprise, plays a significant role in shaping our olfactory identities. Perfumes and colognes are marketed as a means of enhancing our attractiveness, expressing our individuality, and achieving social success. The advertising campaigns for these products often rely on stereotypical representations of gender, sexuality, and social class, reinforcing existing power dynamics and shaping our olfactory preferences.

Smellscapes and the Politics of Place:

The olfactory landscape of a place can be shaped by political and economic forces. Industrial pollution, for example, can create noxious smells that disproportionately affect marginalized communities. The siting of polluting industries in low-income neighborhoods is a form of environmental racism, exposing residents to harmful air pollutants and diminishing their quality of life.

Conversely, the creation of pleasant smellscapes can be used to enhance the image and economic value of a place. Urban planners and developers often use landscaping, public art, and even artificial scents to create attractive and inviting public spaces. The manipulation of smell in these contexts raises questions about who benefits from these olfactory interventions and who is excluded.

Olfactory Citizenship and the Right to Breathe Clean Air:

The right to breathe clean air is a fundamental human right, yet it is often unequally distributed. Environmental pollution, industrial emissions, and agricultural practices can create harmful smells that disproportionately affect vulnerable populations, including children, the elderly, and people with respiratory illnesses.

The concept of olfactory citizenship recognizes that access to clean air and a healthy smellscape is essential for full participation in society. It calls for greater attention to the olfactory dimensions of environmental justice and the need to protect vulnerable communities from the harmful effects of air pollution.

Conclusion:

The politics of smell are complex and multifaceted. Smell has been used as a tool of power and control, a marker of social status and identity, and a means of shaping the environment to reflect dominant ideologies. However, smell has also been used as a form of resistance and subversion, a way of challenging power structures and raising awareness of social injustices. As we become more aware of the profound influence of smell on our lives, we must also become more attuned to the ethical and political dimensions of our olfactory experiences.

Chapter Three: Smellscapes and Social Justice: Environmental Racism and the Right to Breathe Clean Air

The air we breathe is not just a biological necessity; it is a shared resource, a fundamental element of our environment, and a powerful force that shapes our daily lives. The quality of the air we breathe, including its olfactory dimensions, is intimately linked to our health, well-being, and social justice. This chapter explores the concept of smellscapes, the complex olfactory environments that we inhabit, and how these smellscapes are often shaped by social, economic, and political forces that create and perpetuate environmental injustices.

Smellscapes: The Olfactory Environment:

A smellscape is a collection of smells that characterize a particular place. It is the olfactory equivalent of a landscape, a sonic environment, or a visual scene. Smellscapes can be natural or artificial, pleasant or unpleasant, familiar or unfamiliar. They can evoke memories, trigger emotions, and shape our perceptions of a place.

Natural smellscapes are shaped by the presence of plants, animals, and geological formations. The smell of pine needles in a forest, the salty tang of the ocean, or the earthy aroma of a freshly plowed field are all examples of natural smellscapes. Artificial smellscapes, on the other hand, are created by human activities, such as industrial emissions, traffic exhaust, or the use of fragrances in consumer products.

Smellscapes can be dynamic and ever-changing, influenced by factors such as weather patterns, seasonal variations, and human activities. The smellscape of a city, for example, might change throughout the day, with the morning air carrying the aroma of freshly brewed coffee and pastries, giving way to the smell of car exhaust and street food during the midday rush, and ending with the lingering scent of restaurant kitchens and urban nightlife in the evening.

Environmental Racism and the Unequal Distribution of Smell:

The right to breathe clean air is a fundamental human right, yet it is often unequally distributed. Environmental racism, a form of environmental injustice, refers to the disproportionate exposure of marginalized communities, particularly communities of color and low-income communities, to environmental hazards, including air pollution and noxious smells.

Historically, polluting industries, landfills, and waste treatment facilities have been disproportionately located in or near communities of color and low-income communities. This practice, often driven by economic and political factors, has resulted in these communities bearing the brunt of the negative health and environmental impacts of these facilities, including exposure to harmful air pollutants and unpleasant smells.

The smellscapes of these communities are often characterized by the presence of industrial emissions, sewage odors, and other noxious smells. These smells can have a significant impact on the quality of life of residents, leading to respiratory problems, headaches, nausea, and psychological distress. They can also stigmatize these communities, reinforcing negative stereotypes and contributing to social isolation.

The Case of "Cancer Alley":

One of the most well-known examples of environmental racism in the United States is the case of "Cancer Alley," an 85-mile stretch of land along the Mississippi River between Baton Rouge and New Orleans, Louisiana. This area is home to a high concentration of petrochemical plants and refineries, and it has some of the highest cancer rates in the country.

The residents of Cancer Alley, many of whom are African American, have long complained about the noxious smells emanating from these industrial facilities. The smells, often described as sulfurous, chemical, or metallic, are a constant reminder of the environmental hazards that they face on a daily basis. Studies have shown that these smells are not just unpleasant; they are also associated with a range of health problems, including respiratory illnesses, cardiovascular disease, and cancer.

The case of Cancer Alley highlights the intersection of race, poverty, and environmental injustice. The residents of this community have been disproportionately exposed to industrial pollution and noxious smells, leading to a higher incidence of health problems and a diminished quality of life. Their struggle for environmental justice has been a long and difficult one, but it has also inspired other communities across the country to fight for their right to breathe clean air.

The Smell of Inequality: Hog Farming and Environmental Justice:

Another example of environmental racism can be found in the hog farming industry. Large-scale hog farms, also known as Concentrated Animal Feeding Operations (CAFOs), are a major source of air pollution and noxious smells. These farms confine thousands of pigs in close quarters, producing vast quantities of manure and other waste products.

The smell of hog manure, often described as overpowering, nauseating, and ammonia-like, can travel for miles, affecting the quality of life of nearby residents. Studies have shown that exposure to hog farm odors is associated with a range of health problems, including respiratory illnesses, headaches, nausea, and stress.

Hog farms are disproportionately located in or near communities of color and low-income communities. This siting pattern reflects a history of racial discrimination and economic inequality in the agricultural industry. The residents of these communities have often been denied the opportunity to participate in decision-making processes regarding the location of hog farms, and they have borne the brunt of the negative environmental impacts of these facilities.

The Fight for Olfactory Justice:

The fight for environmental justice includes the fight for olfactory justice, the right to live in an environment free from noxious smells and other olfactory hazards. Communities across the country are organizing to challenge the siting of polluting industries and other facilities that produce unpleasant smells in their neighborhoods. They are demanding greater transparency and accountability from government agencies and corporations, and they are advocating for policies that protect the right to breathe clean air for all.

Olfactory justice is not just about eliminating unpleasant smells; it is also about recognizing the cultural and social significance of smell. Smells can evoke memories, trigger emotions, and shape our perceptions of a place. The destruction of traditional smellscapes, whether through industrial pollution or the homogenization of urban environments, can have a profound impact on the cultural identity and well-being of communities.

The Role of Government and Industry:

Government agencies and corporations have a responsibility to address the problem of environmental racism and olfactory injustice. They must take steps to reduce air pollution and noxious smells from industrial facilities, landfills, and other sources. They must also ensure that marginalized communities are not disproportionately exposed to these environmental hazards.

Environmental regulations, such as the Clean Air Act, play an important role in protecting the right to breathe clean air. These regulations must be enforced effectively, and they should be updated to reflect the latest scientific understanding of the health impacts of air pollution and noxious smells.

Corporations also have a responsibility to operate in a manner that minimizes environmental impacts, including the production of noxious smells. They should invest in technologies that reduce emissions and odors, and they should engage in meaningful dialogue with communities that are affected by their operations.

The Importance of Community Engagement:

Community engagement is essential in addressing the problem of environmental racism and olfactory injustice. Affected communities must be involved in decision-making processes regarding the siting of polluting industries and other facilities that produce unpleasant smells. They must also be given the opportunity to participate in the development and implementation of solutions.

Community-based participatory research, a collaborative approach to research that involves community members in all stages of the research process, can be a powerful tool for understanding the impacts of environmental hazards on communities and for developing effective solutions. This approach can help to ensure that research is relevant to the needs of the community and that the results are used to inform policy and practice.

Olfactory Literacy and Environmental Awareness:

Promoting olfactory literacy, the ability to identify, understand, and appreciate smells, can play an important role in raising awareness of environmental issues and fostering a sense of environmental stewardship. Educating people about the sources and impacts of air pollution and noxious smells can empower them to take action to protect their own health and the health of their communities.

Olfactory art, which uses smell as a medium of artistic expression, can also be a powerful tool for raising awareness of environmental issues and promoting social change. Smell artists can create olfactory installations that evoke the smells of polluted environments or that highlight the beauty and fragility of natural smellscapes.

Conclusion:

The air we breathe is a shared resource, and the right to breathe clean air is a fundamental human right. Environmental racism and olfactory injustice are serious problems that disproportionately affect marginalized communities. Addressing these problems requires a multi-faceted approach that involves government agencies, corporations, and communities working together. By promoting olfactory literacy, raising awareness of environmental issues, and advocating for policies that protect the right to breathe clean air for all, we can create a more just and sustainable olfactory environment for all.

Chapter Four: The Fragrant Divide: Class, Status, and the Cultural Construction of Smell

Smell, despite its invisibility, has played a powerful role in shaping social hierarchies and reinforcing class distinctions throughout history. The way we perceive and interpret smells is not solely based on their inherent qualities but is profoundly influenced by cultural norms, social expectations, and economic realities. This chapter delves into the intricate relationship between smell, class, and status, exploring how olfactory perceptions have been used to define social boundaries, establish hierarchies of taste, and perpetuate inequalities.

The Olfactory Elite and the Democratization of Fragrance:

In many societies, the ability to control and manipulate smells has been a marker of social status and privilege. In ancient Egypt, perfumes and incense were reserved for the elite, signifying their power, wealth, and proximity to the divine. The Egyptians believed that pleasant fragrances were a manifestation of the gods and that by adorning themselves with these scents, they could enhance their own status and garner favor with the deities. Similarly, in ancient Rome, the use of perfumes and spices was a luxury enjoyed primarily by the wealthy, while the lower classes were often associated with the stench of poverty and manual labor.

The association of pleasant smells with the upper classes persisted throughout the Middle Ages and into the Renaissance. In Europe, the use of perfumes and spices became a symbol of wealth and refinement, with elaborate fragrance rituals and the importation of exotic scents from distant lands serving as a testament to one's social standing. The lower classes, on the other hand, were often relegated to a world of unpleasant smells, associated with unsanitary living conditions, manual labor, and the lack of access to hygiene products.

However, the 18th and 19th centuries witnessed a gradual democratization of fragrance, as advancements in chemistry and manufacturing made perfumes and other scented products more accessible to the masses. The rise of the middle class and the increasing emphasis on personal hygiene also contributed to the growing demand for fragrances. This democratization of smell did not, however, erase the olfactory hierarchies that had been established over centuries. Instead, it led to the development of new forms of olfactory distinction, with different fragrances and scent profiles becoming associated with different social classes and lifestyles.

The Smell of Status: Luxury Perfumes and the Aspiration for Refinement:

The fragrance industry, a multi-billion dollar global enterprise, plays a significant role in shaping our olfactory perceptions and reinforcing social hierarchies. Luxury perfume brands often cultivate an aura of exclusivity and sophistication, associating their products with wealth, status, and refinement. These brands use elaborate marketing campaigns, featuring celebrities, high-fashion imagery, and evocative narratives, to create a sense of aspiration and desire among consumers.

The price tag of a luxury perfume can itself be a marker of status, with some fragrances costing hundreds or even thousands of dollars per bottle. The use of rare and exotic ingredients, such as oud wood, ambergris, and certain floral extracts, further contributes to the perception of luxury and exclusivity. The fragrance industry also employs the language of art and connoisseurship to elevate the status of its products, with perfumers often referred to as "noses" and fragrances described in terms of their complexity, artistry, and olfactory "notes."

This association of luxury perfumes with status and refinement can create a sense of olfactory insecurity among those who cannot afford these products. The inability to access or appreciate these fragrances can be perceived as a sign of lower social standing or a lack of sophistication. This can lead to a form of olfactory anxiety, where individuals feel pressured to conform to the dominant olfactory norms and acquire the "right" scents to enhance their social status.

Olfactory Stereotypes and the Stigmatization of Poverty:

While luxury perfumes are associated with wealth and refinement, certain smells have been historically linked to poverty and lower social classes. The smell of sweat, body odor, and unsanitary living conditions has often been used to stigmatize and marginalize the poor. This association of smell with poverty can have profound social and psychological consequences, reinforcing negative stereotypes, perpetuating discrimination, and contributing to social exclusion.

The stigmatization of poverty through smell can manifest in various ways. For example, individuals from lower socioeconomic backgrounds may be subjected to olfactory discrimination in housing, employment, and social interactions. They may be perceived as less hygienic, less intelligent, or less deserving of respect based solely on their perceived smell. This can lead to internalized stigma, where individuals from marginalized communities begin to accept and internalize the negative stereotypes associated with their social class and their perceived smell.

The media often plays a role in perpetuating olfactory stereotypes, portraying individuals from lower socioeconomic backgrounds as unkempt, smelly, and uncultured. This can further reinforce the association of poverty with unpleasant smells and contribute to the social and psychological marginalization of these communities.

The Smell of Labor and the Devaluation of Manual Work:

Certain smells have also been associated with manual labor and the working class. The smell of sweat, grease, and industrial chemicals has often been used to distinguish the working class from the "cleaner" and more "refined" upper classes. This olfactory distinction can reflect and reinforce the devaluation of manual labor and the social hierarchy that places intellectual work above physical work.

In many societies, manual laborers are often relegated to the margins of society, both physically and symbolically. They are often employed in jobs that involve exposure to unpleasant smells, such as sanitation work, factory work, and agricultural labor. This exposure to unpleasant smells can further contribute to the stigmatization of these occupations and the devaluation of the workers who perform them.

The smell of labor can also be a source of pride and identity for some workers. For example, the smell of freshly cut wood might be associated with the skill and craftsmanship of a carpenter, while the smell of engine oil might be a badge of honor for a mechanic. However, these positive associations with the smell of labor are often overshadowed by the broader social stigma attached to manual work and the smells associated with it.

Olfactory Gentrification and the Displacement of Smell Cultures:

The process of gentrification, the transformation of working-class neighborhoods into more affluent communities, can also have olfactory dimensions. As wealthier residents move into these neighborhoods, they often bring with them different olfactory expectations and preferences. This can lead to the displacement of traditional smell cultures, as businesses and residents catering to the new demographic introduce new smellscapes that reflect the tastes and preferences of the affluent newcomers.

For example, the opening of upscale restaurants, artisanal coffee shops, and boutique stores in a gentrifying neighborhood might introduce new smells that are perceived as more desirable or sophisticated by the new residents. These new smellscapes can clash with the existing olfactory environment, displacing the smells associated with traditional businesses, such as auto repair shops, laundromats, and ethnic food markets.

This olfactory gentrification can further contribute to the social and economic marginalization of the original residents, who may feel alienated by the changing smellscape and the influx of new businesses and residents who do not share their olfactory preferences. The displacement of traditional smell cultures can also erode the sense of place and community identity that is often tied to the familiar smells of a neighborhood.

The Smell of "Clean": Hygiene, Morality, and Social Control:

The concept of "cleanliness" and its associated smells have also been used to reinforce social hierarchies and exert social control. In the 19th century, the rise of the public health movement and the growing emphasis on personal hygiene led to the association of cleanliness with morality and social respectability. The use of soap, deodorant, and other hygiene products became a marker of social status and a means of distinguishing oneself from the "unclean" and "uncivilized" lower classes.

This association of cleanliness with morality and social status persists in many societies today. The smell of "clean," often associated with the scent of laundry detergent, bleach, and disinfectant, can be perceived as a sign of order, discipline, and respectability. Conversely, the absence of this smell, or the presence of smells associated with sweat, body odor, or dirt, can be perceived as a sign of deviance, laziness, or lack of self-respect.

The emphasis on cleanliness and its associated smells can be used as a tool of social control, particularly in institutional settings such as schools, hospitals, and prisons. The enforcement of strict hygiene standards, often accompanied by the use of strong-smelling cleaning products, can be a way of regulating the behavior of individuals and maintaining order within these institutions.

The Smell of "Otherness": Class, Ethnicity, and Olfactory Prejudice:

Smell has also been used to construct and reinforce social boundaries between different ethnic and cultural groups. The perception of "otherness" can often be mediated through smell, with unfamiliar or "foreign" smells being perceived as threatening, repulsive, or indicative of lower social status.

Throughout history, certain ethnic and racial groups have been stereotyped based on their perceived smell. For example, in the 19th century, European colonizers often described the smell of indigenous populations as "primitive," "uncivilized," or "animalistic." These olfactory stereotypes were used to justify the subjugation and exploitation of these populations, reinforcing the notion of European superiority and the "civilizing mission" of colonialism.

Olfactory prejudice can manifest in various forms, from subtle expressions of discomfort or avoidance to overt acts of discrimination. Individuals from marginalized ethnic or cultural groups may be subjected to olfactory microaggressions, such as being told that they "smell different" or that their food has a "strong" smell. These microaggressions can contribute to feelings of alienation, shame, and social isolation.

Challenging the Fragrant Divide: Olfactory Justice and Social Change:

The fragrant divide, the unequal distribution of olfactory resources and the perpetuation of olfactory stereotypes, is a form of social injustice. Challenging this divide requires a multi-faceted approach that addresses the underlying social, economic, and cultural factors that contribute to olfactory inequality.

Promoting olfactory literacy, the ability to identify, understand, and appreciate a diverse range of smells, can help to challenge olfactory stereotypes and foster a greater appreciation for different smell cultures. Educating people about the cultural and historical significance of smell can also help to dismantle the notion that certain smells are inherently superior or inferior to others.

Addressing the issue of environmental racism, the disproportionate exposure of marginalized communities to environmental hazards, including noxious smells, is also crucial for achieving olfactory justice. Ensuring that all communities have access to clean air and a healthy smellscape is essential for promoting social equity and well-being.

The fragrance industry also has a role to play in challenging the fragrant divide. By promoting greater diversity and inclusivity in its marketing campaigns, product development, and hiring practices, the industry can help to dismantle olfactory stereotypes and create a more equitable and just olfactory landscape.

Ultimately, challenging the fragrant divide requires a fundamental shift in our understanding of smell and its relationship to social hierarchies. We must move away from a hierarchical view of smell, where certain smells are associated with status and privilege while others are stigmatized and marginalized. Instead, we must embrace a more inclusive and equitable approach to smell, recognizing the diversity of olfactory experiences and the cultural significance of smell in different communities.

Chapter Five: The Ethics of Fragrance: Marketing, Manipulation, and the Olfactory Consumer

The fragrance industry, a multi-billion dollar global enterprise, wields considerable influence over our olfactory experiences. From the perfumes and colognes we wear to the scented products that fill our homes and workplaces, the industry shapes our perceptions of what smells are desirable, appropriate, and even necessary. This chapter explores the ethical dimensions of the fragrance industry's practices, examining how marketing strategies, product formulations, and industry regulations impact consumer choice, health, and well-being.

The Allure of Fragrance: Marketing and the Creation of Olfactory Desire:

Fragrance advertising often relies on aspirational imagery and evocative language to create a sense of desire and allure around its products. Perfumes and colognes are marketed as a means of enhancing one's attractiveness, boosting confidence, and achieving social success. Advertisements often feature celebrities, high-fashion models, and exotic locales, suggesting that the use of a particular fragrance can transform one's life and social standing.

These marketing campaigns often tap into deep-seated psychological desires, such as the desire for love, acceptance, and belonging. Fragrances are presented as a means of achieving these desires, promising to make the wearer more attractive, confident, and desirable to others. This can be particularly effective in a society that places a high value on physical appearance and social status.

However, the idealized images and promises presented in fragrance advertising can also create unrealistic expectations and a sense of olfactory insecurity among consumers. The inability to achieve the idealized lifestyle or level of attractiveness portrayed in these advertisements can lead to feelings of inadequacy and a pressure to conform to the dominant olfactory norms.

The Language of Scent: Marketing Jargon and the Illusion of Expertise:

The fragrance industry often employs a specialized vocabulary to describe its products, creating a sense of exclusivity and expertise that can be both alluring and intimidating to consumers. Terms like "top notes," "heart notes," "base notes," "sillage," and "olfactory pyramid" are used to describe the composition and evolution of a fragrance over time. These terms, while meaningful to perfumers and fragrance enthusiasts, can be confusing and opaque to the average consumer.

This specialized language can create a power imbalance between the fragrance industry and consumers. Consumers may feel unqualified to judge the quality or appropriateness of a fragrance based on their own olfactory perceptions, relying instead on the expertise and pronouncements of the industry. This can lead to a sense of dependence on the industry's pronouncements and a reluctance to challenge its marketing claims.

The Science of Scent: Product Formulations and the Manipulation of Olfactory Responses:

Fragrance formulations are complex mixtures of synthetic and natural ingredients, carefully crafted to elicit specific emotional and physiological responses. Perfumers use their knowledge of fragrance chemistry and human olfactory perception to create scents that evoke feelings of happiness, relaxation, sensuality, or even nostalgia.

These formulations can be highly effective in manipulating consumer behavior. Studies have shown that certain scents can influence mood, memory, and even purchasing decisions. For example, the smell of lavender has been shown to have a calming effect, while the smell of citrus can be energizing. Retailers often use scent marketing, the strategic use of fragrance in retail environments, to create a more inviting atmosphere and encourage shoppers to linger and spend more money.

However, the manipulation of olfactory responses raises ethical concerns about consumer autonomy and the potential for exploitation. Consumers may be unaware of the extent to which their olfactory perceptions and behaviors are being influenced by fragrance formulations. This raises questions about the transparency of the fragrance industry's practices and the need for greater consumer awareness and education.

The Hidden Ingredients: Fragrance Allergens and the Right to Know:

Fragrance formulations often contain a wide range of chemicals, some of which can be allergens or irritants. These chemicals are not always listed on product labels, as fragrance formulas are often considered trade secrets. This lack of transparency can pose health risks for consumers, particularly those with sensitivities or allergies to certain fragrance ingredients.

Fragrance allergens can cause a range of adverse reactions, including skin rashes, headaches, respiratory problems, and even asthma attacks. The prevalence of fragrance allergies is increasing, with some estimates suggesting that up to 3% of the population may be affected. This raises concerns about the safety of fragrance products and the need for greater transparency in labeling and ingredient disclosure.

The right to know what is in the products we use is a fundamental consumer right. Consumers have a right to make informed decisions about the products they purchase and use, and this includes the right to know about the potential health risks associated with fragrance ingredients. Greater transparency in fragrance labeling would empower consumers to make choices that are consistent with their own health and well-being.

The Regulation of Fragrance: Balancing Industry Interests and Consumer Protection:

The fragrance industry is subject to a patchwork of regulations, both domestically and internationally. These regulations vary in their scope and effectiveness, and there are ongoing debates about the adequacy of existing regulations to protect consumer health and the environment.

In the United States, the Food and Drug Administration (FDA) has limited authority to regulate fragrance ingredients. The FDA's primary focus is on ensuring the safety of cosmetics and other personal care products, but it does not require fragrance manufacturers to disclose the specific ingredients in their formulations. This lack of transparency makes it difficult for consumers to identify and avoid fragrance allergens or other potentially harmful ingredients.

In Europe, the European Union (EU) has stricter regulations on fragrance ingredients. The EU's Cosmetics Regulation requires fragrance manufacturers to disclose 26 specific fragrance allergens on product labels if they are present at concentrations above certain thresholds. This greater transparency allows consumers to make more informed choices about the fragrance products they purchase and use.

However, even in the EU, there are concerns about the adequacy of existing regulations. Some consumer advocates argue that the list of disclosed allergens is not comprehensive enough and that there are other fragrance ingredients that can pose health risks. There are also concerns about the enforcement of existing regulations and the need for greater oversight of the fragrance industry.

The Ethics of Scent Marketing: Manipulation, Consent, and the Public Smellscape:

Scent marketing, the strategic use of fragrance in retail and other environments, raises ethical concerns about the manipulation of consumer behavior and the potential for intrusion into the public smellscape. Retailers often use scent marketing to create a more inviting atmosphere, enhance brand identity, and even influence purchasing decisions.

While some consumers may find scent marketing to be pleasant or even beneficial, others may find it to be intrusive, manipulative, or even harmful. Individuals with sensitivities or allergies to certain fragrance ingredients may experience adverse reactions, and the use of scent marketing in public spaces can limit the ability of individuals to avoid exposure to unwanted smells.

The ethics of scent marketing hinge on the issue of consent. Consumers should have the right to choose whether or not they are exposed to fragrance in retail and other environments. This requires greater transparency about the use of scent marketing and the ability for consumers to opt out of exposure. The use of scent marketing in public spaces should also be carefully considered, taking into account the potential impact on individuals with sensitivities or allergies and the right to a shared public smellscape that is not dominated by commercial interests.

Sustainable Fragrance: Environmental Concerns and the Ethical Sourcing of Ingredients:

The fragrance industry's reliance on natural ingredients, such as essential oils and plant extracts, raises concerns about the environmental impact of fragrance production and the ethical sourcing of these ingredients. The harvesting of certain plant species for fragrance production can contribute to deforestation, habitat loss, and the exploitation of local communities.

For example, the production of sandalwood oil, a popular fragrance ingredient, has led to the overharvesting of sandalwood trees in some regions, threatening the survival of these species. The harvesting of agarwood, another valuable fragrance ingredient, can also have negative environmental impacts, as the trees are often wounded or felled to stimulate the production of the resinous wood that is used in perfumery.

The ethical sourcing of fragrance ingredients requires a commitment to sustainable harvesting practices, fair trade principles, and the protection of biodiversity. Fragrance companies should work with suppliers who are committed to these principles, and they should be transparent about the sourcing of their ingredients. Consumers can also play a role in promoting sustainable fragrance by choosing products that are made with ethically sourced ingredients.

The Future of Fragrance: Ethical Innovation and the Olfactory Consumer:

The fragrance industry is constantly evolving, with new technologies and ingredients emerging that offer both opportunities and challenges for the ethical development and use of fragrance. Biotechnology, for example, is being used to create new fragrance ingredients that are more sustainable and environmentally friendly. Synthetic biology, a field that involves the design and engineering of biological systems, is also being explored as a means of creating new fragrance molecules.

These technological advancements raise ethical questions about the safety and long-term impacts of these new ingredients. There is also a need for greater transparency and consumer education about the use of these technologies in fragrance production.

The future of fragrance will also be shaped by changing consumer preferences and a growing awareness of the ethical dimensions of fragrance production and consumption. Consumers are increasingly demanding transparency about fragrance ingredients, sustainable sourcing practices, and the responsible use of scent marketing. This growing consumer awareness is driving innovation and change within the fragrance industry, as companies seek to meet the demands of a more ethically conscious consumer base.

The ethical challenges facing the fragrance industry are complex and multifaceted. Addressing these challenges requires a collaborative effort between industry stakeholders, regulators, consumer advocates, and researchers. By promoting greater transparency, fostering ethical innovation, and empowering consumers to make informed choices, we can create a more sustainable, just, and fragrant future for all.

Chapter Six: Olfactory Nuisances: Public Space, Private Lives, and the Regulation of Smell

The smells that permeate our environment, both public and private, can be a source of both pleasure and conflict. While certain scents evoke positive emotions and memories, others can be perceived as offensive, intrusive, and even harmful. This chapter explores the concept of olfactory nuisances, examining the tensions that arise when individual olfactory preferences clash with the smellscapes of shared spaces. We will delve into the challenges of regulating smells, the legal frameworks that govern olfactory nuisances, and the ethical considerations that arise when balancing individual rights with the collective well-being.

Defining Olfactory Nuisances: When Smells Cross the Line:

The concept of an olfactory nuisance is inherently subjective and culturally contingent. What one person finds offensive, another may find pleasant or even insignificant. However, certain smells are widely considered to be nuisances, particularly when they are persistent, intense, or interfere with the enjoyment of one's property or public spaces.

Common examples of olfactory nuisances include:

- **Industrial emissions:** Factories, power plants, and other industrial facilities can release a variety of pollutants into the air, including noxious smells that can travel for miles.

- **Agricultural odors:** Large-scale animal farms, particularly hog farms and poultry farms, can produce strong and pervasive odors that affect the quality of life of nearby residents.

- **Waste management facilities:** Landfills, sewage treatment plants, and other waste management facilities can generate unpleasant smells that can be a source of nuisance for surrounding communities.

- **Commercial activities:** Restaurants, bakeries, and other businesses can produce smells that, while not necessarily harmful, can be perceived as intrusive or offensive by some individuals.

- **Residential activities:** Smoking, cooking, pet odors, and other residential activities can also be a source of olfactory nuisance, particularly in multi-unit dwellings.

The determination of whether a smell constitutes a nuisance often depends on a variety of factors, including the intensity and duration of the smell, the frequency of exposure, the sensitivity of the individual, and the context in which the smell occurs. For example, a strong smell of cooking spices might be considered acceptable in a restaurant district but might be perceived as a nuisance in a residential neighborhood.

The Public-Private Divide: Smellscapes in Shared Spaces:

The regulation of smells becomes particularly challenging in shared spaces, where individual olfactory preferences must be balanced with the rights and freedoms of others. Public spaces, such as parks, streets, and sidewalks, are often subject to a wide range of smells emanating from various sources, including traffic exhaust, street vendors, and passersby.

The smellscapes of public spaces can be a reflection of the diversity and vibrancy of a community. However, they can also be a source of conflict, particularly when certain smells are perceived as offensive or intrusive. For example, the smell of cigarette smoke can be a source of nuisance for non-smokers, while the smell of strong perfumes or colognes can trigger allergic reactions or sensitivities in some individuals.

Private spaces, such as homes and apartments, also present challenges for the regulation of smells. While individuals have a greater degree of control over the smellscape within their own homes, they must also be mindful of the potential impact of their olfactory choices on their neighbors. For example, cooking strong-smelling foods or using excessive amounts of air freshener can create smells that permeate through walls and ventilation systems, affecting the quality of life of those living nearby.

Legal Frameworks for Regulating Olfactory Nuisances:

The legal frameworks for regulating olfactory nuisances vary across jurisdictions, but they typically involve a combination of common law principles, statutory regulations, and local ordinances. Common law principles, based on legal precedents and judicial interpretations, often provide a basis for nuisance claims, allowing individuals to seek redress for unreasonable interference with the use and enjoyment of their property.

Statutory regulations, enacted by legislative bodies, may establish specific standards for air quality and odor control, particularly in relation to industrial emissions and agricultural operations. Local ordinances, enacted by municipal governments, can also address specific olfactory nuisances, such as restrictions on smoking in public places or regulations on the use of outdoor grills and fire pits.

The enforcement of olfactory nuisance laws can be challenging, as the subjective nature of smell makes it difficult to establish objective standards for what constitutes a nuisance. In many cases, the resolution of olfactory nuisance disputes relies on negotiation and compromise between the parties involved. Mediation and other alternative dispute resolution mechanisms can also be effective in resolving these conflicts.

The Right to Breathe Clean Air: Environmental Justice and Olfactory Equity:

The right to breathe clean air, including freedom from noxious smells, is increasingly recognized as a fundamental human right. Environmental justice movements have highlighted the disproportionate burden of air pollution and olfactory nuisances borne by marginalized communities, particularly communities of color and low-income communities.

These communities are often located in close proximity to polluting industries, waste management facilities, and other sources of unpleasant smells. This exposure to noxious smells can have significant impacts on their health, well-being, and quality of life. Environmental justice advocates argue that all communities have a right to a healthy and pleasant smellscape, regardless of their socioeconomic status or racial background.

Olfactory equity, a concept that builds upon the principles of environmental justice, seeks to ensure that all individuals have access to a clean and pleasant olfactory environment. This includes addressing the unequal distribution of olfactory nuisances, promoting community participation in decision-making processes related to smell, and recognizing the cultural significance of smell in different communities.

The Challenges of Measuring and Regulating Smell:

One of the major challenges in regulating olfactory nuisances is the difficulty of objectively measuring and quantifying smell. Unlike other environmental pollutants, such as noise or particulate matter, smell is a subjective sensory experience that can vary greatly from person to person.

While there are technologies available for measuring the concentration of certain odor-causing compounds in the air, these measurements do not necessarily correlate with the perceived intensity or offensiveness of a smell. The human olfactory system is highly sensitive and complex, and the perception of smell can be influenced by a variety of factors, including individual sensitivities, psychological factors, and cultural norms.

This subjectivity of smell makes it difficult to establish objective standards for what constitutes an olfactory nuisance. Regulatory agencies often rely on odor panels, groups of trained individuals who assess the intensity and character of smells, to make subjective judgments about the offensiveness of odors. However, the use of odor panels can be expensive and time-consuming, and their judgments can be influenced by individual biases and cultural backgrounds.

Technological Solutions for Odor Control:

Advances in technology are providing new tools for mitigating and controlling olfactory nuisances. These technologies can be broadly categorized into three main approaches:

- **Source reduction:** This approach focuses on reducing the amount of odor-causing compounds released at the source. This can involve changes in industrial processes, the use of cleaner fuels, or the implementation of waste management practices that minimize odor emissions.

- **Odor treatment:** This approach involves using technologies to remove or neutralize odor-causing compounds from the air. This can include techniques such as biofiltration, activated carbon adsorption, and chemical scrubbing.

- **Odor masking:** This approach involves using fragrances or other masking agents to cover up or neutralize unpleasant smells. This can be effective in certain situations, but it is important to consider the potential impact on individuals with sensitivities or allergies to fragrance ingredients.

The choice of odor control technology depends on a variety of factors, including the type and intensity of the odor, the cost-effectiveness of the technology, and the potential environmental impacts. In many cases, a combination of different approaches may be necessary to effectively address an olfactory nuisance.

The Ethics of Olfactory Intervention: Balancing Individual Rights and the Common Good:

The regulation of smells raises ethical questions about the balance between individual rights and the common good. On the one hand, individuals have a right to enjoy their property and public spaces without being subjected to unreasonable interference from unpleasant smells. On the other hand, the restriction of certain smells may infringe on the rights and freedoms of others, such as the right to engage in certain commercial activities or the right to express oneself through the use of fragrance.

The ethical framework for regulating smells should be guided by principles of fairness, proportionality, and respect for individual autonomy. Restrictions on smells should be based on a clear demonstration of harm or nuisance, and they should be tailored to address the specific olfactory problem at hand. The use of punitive measures, such as fines or imprisonment, should be reserved for egregious violations of olfactory nuisance laws.

Transparency and community participation are also essential in the ethical regulation of smells. Individuals and communities should be informed about the potential impacts of olfactory nuisances and the measures being taken to address them. They should also be given the opportunity to participate in decision-making processes related to the regulation of smells in their communities.

The Evolving Smellscape: Adapting to a Changing Olfactory Environment:

The smellscapes of our world are constantly evolving, shaped by technological advancements, demographic shifts, and changing cultural norms. As we become more aware of the impact of smells on our health, well-being, and social interactions, we must also adapt our approaches to regulating smells to reflect these changing realities.

The development of new technologies for measuring and controlling smells, coupled with a growing understanding of the human olfactory system, offers opportunities for more effective and nuanced approaches to olfactory nuisance regulation. The integration of olfactory considerations into urban planning and

41

design can also help to create more pleasant and equitable smellscapes in our cities and communities.

Ultimately, the regulation of smells is a complex and evolving challenge that requires a nuanced understanding of the science of olfaction, the legal frameworks governing nuisance, and the ethical considerations that arise when balancing individual rights with the common good. By fostering greater olfactory literacy, promoting community dialogue, and embracing innovative solutions, we can create a more harmonious and fragrant world for all.

Chapter Seven: The Smell of Fear: Olfactory Security and the Biopolitics of Surveillance

Our sense of smell, often operating beneath the level of conscious awareness, plays a powerful role in shaping our perceptions of safety and danger. From the primal fear evoked by the smell of smoke to the subtle cues that alert us to potential threats, our olfactory system acts as an early warning system, triggering physiological and behavioral responses that can be crucial for survival. This chapter explores the intersection of smell and security, examining how olfactory cues are used in surveillance technologies, the ethical implications of deploying these technologies, and the potential for smell to be weaponized in the pursuit of security and control.

Olfactory Surveillance: Sniffing Out Threats in a World of Danger:

The use of smell in security and surveillance is not a new phenomenon. For centuries, dogs have been employed for their keen sense of smell to detect explosives, drugs, and other contraband. However, recent advancements in technology have expanded the possibilities of olfactory surveillance, enabling the development of sophisticated devices and systems that can detect and analyze a wide range of smells with unprecedented accuracy and speed.

These technologies have found applications in various security contexts, including:

- **Airport security:** Olfactory sensors are being deployed in airports to detect explosives, narcotics, and other prohibited substances. These sensors can analyze the air for trace amounts of volatile organic compounds (VOCs) that are associated with these substances, providing a noninvasive and rapid means of screening passengers and luggage.

- **Border control:** Olfactory surveillance is also being used at border crossings to detect smuggled goods, including drugs, weapons, and agricultural products that may pose biosecurity risks.

- **Law enforcement:** Police and other law enforcement agencies are using olfactory sensors to detect hidden drugs, explosives, and even human remains. These sensors can be used in conjunction with drug-sniffing dogs to enhance the effectiveness of search operations.

- **Environmental monitoring:** Olfactory sensors are being used to monitor air quality, detect leaks of hazardous materials, and identify sources of pollution. This information can be used to protect public health and the environment.

- **Food safety:** Olfactory sensors are being developed to detect food spoilage, contamination, and adulteration. This technology can help to ensure the safety and quality of our food supply.

The Biopolitics of Smell: Security, Control, and the Olfactory Body:

The deployment of olfactory surveillance technologies raises ethical concerns about the potential for these technologies to be used for purposes beyond their stated security objectives. The concept of biopolitics, developed by French philosopher Michel Foucault, refers to the ways in which power is exercised over the bodies and lives of individuals and populations. Olfactory surveillance, by targeting the smells emanating from our bodies and our environments, can be seen as a form of biopolitical control.

The use of olfactory sensors to detect emotions, such as fear or anxiety, raises concerns about the potential for these technologies to be used for discriminatory purposes. For example, individuals who exhibit signs of anxiety or fear when passing through airport security might be subjected to increased scrutiny or profiling based solely on their olfactory profile. This could lead to the targeting of certain groups, such as ethnic minorities or individuals with mental health conditions, based on unfounded assumptions about their potential threat level.

The collection and analysis of olfactory data also raises privacy concerns. Our body odor, a complex mixture of VOCs, can reveal a wealth of information about our health, diet, emotional state, and even our genetic predispositions. The widespread deployment of olfactory sensors in public spaces could lead to the creation of vast olfactory databases, potentially revealing intimate details about our lives without our knowledge or consent.

The potential for olfactory data to be used for commercial purposes, such as targeted advertising or insurance risk assessment, also raises ethical concerns. The commodification of our olfactory data could lead to a new form of data exploitation, where our most intimate and personal information is used for profit without our knowledge or control.

The Weaponization of Smell: Olfactory Warfare and the Ethics of Sensory Disruption:

Smell has also been used as a weapon of war and social control. Malodorants, chemicals that produce highly unpleasant smells, have been used as a form of crowd control, riot suppression, and even torture. "Skunk bombs," for example, which emit a foul-smelling liquid, have been used by law enforcement agencies to disperse protesters and control unruly crowds.

The use of malodorants in these contexts raises serious ethical concerns about the potential for psychological harm and the violation of human rights. The deliberate infliction of unpleasant smells can cause nausea, vomiting, headaches, and psychological distress. The use of malodorants as a form of torture has been condemned by human rights organizations as a violation of the prohibition against cruel, inhuman, and degrading treatment.

The development of more sophisticated olfactory weapons, such as odor-based incapacitants or "olfactory bombs," raises further ethical concerns. These weapons could be used to disable or disorient individuals without causing lasting physical harm. However, the potential for these weapons to be used for indiscriminate or malicious purposes, such as targeting civilians or suppressing dissent, raises serious questions about their ethical permissibility.

The Smell of Fear and the Politics of Anxiety:

The manipulation of smell can also be used to create and reinforce a climate of fear and anxiety. The association of certain smells with danger, such as the smell of smoke or the smell of explosives, can trigger primal fear responses and heighten our sense of vulnerability. This can be exploited by those in power to justify increased security measures, surveillance, and social control.

The "war on terror," for example, has been accompanied by a heightened awareness of the potential for terrorist attacks using chemical or biological weapons. This has led to the deployment of olfactory sensors in public spaces, such as airports and train stations, to detect the presence of these weapons. While these measures may be justified in certain contexts, they can also contribute to a climate of fear and suspicion, potentially eroding civil liberties and creating a sense of unease in public life.

The media often plays a role in amplifying the smell of fear, sensationalizing the threat of terrorism and other dangers and highlighting the potential for olfactory surveillance to detect these threats. This can create a self-reinforcing cycle, where the heightened perception of risk leads to increased demand for security measures, which in turn further amplifies the sense of fear and anxiety.

Olfactory Citizenship and the Right to a Safe and Pleasant Smellscape:

The right to a safe and pleasant smellscape is an essential component of olfactory citizenship. This right encompasses both the freedom from noxious smells and other olfactory hazards and the ability to enjoy and appreciate the diverse smellscapes of our world.

Protecting the right to a safe smellscape requires addressing the issue of environmental racism, the disproportionate exposure of marginalized communities to environmental hazards, including noxious smells. Ensuring that all communities have access to clean air and a healthy smellscape is essential for promoting social equity and well-being.

The right to a pleasant smellscape also entails recognizing the cultural and social significance of smell. Smells can evoke memories, trigger emotions, and shape our perceptions of a place. The destruction of traditional smellscapes, whether through industrial pollution or the homogenization of urban environments, can have a profound impact on the cultural identity and well-being of communities.

Promoting olfactory literacy, the ability to identify, understand, and appreciate a diverse range of smells, can also contribute to a safer and more pleasant smellscape. Educating people about the sources and impacts of air pollution and noxious smells can empower them to take action to protect their own health and the health of their communities.

The Future of Olfactory Security: Balancing Security Needs with Ethical Concerns:

The future of olfactory security will be shaped by ongoing advancements in technology, evolving security threats, and changing societal values. As olfactory surveillance technologies become more sophisticated and widely deployed, it is essential to address the ethical concerns raised by these technologies and to ensure that they are used in a manner that respects human rights, privacy, and the common good.

Greater transparency and accountability are needed in the development and deployment of olfactory surveillance technologies. The public should be informed about the capabilities and limitations of these technologies, the purposes for which they are being used, and the safeguards in place to protect privacy and prevent misuse.

Independent oversight and regulation are also essential to ensure that olfactory surveillance technologies are used responsibly and ethically. Regulatory frameworks should be established to govern the collection, storage, and use of olfactory data, and mechanisms should be put in place to address potential biases and discriminatory impacts.

The development of ethical guidelines for the use of olfactory surveillance technologies is also crucial. These guidelines should address issues such as informed consent, data security, and the prevention of misuse. The involvement of ethicists, legal scholars, and civil society organizations in the development of these guidelines is essential to ensure that they reflect a broad range of perspectives and values.

The future of olfactory security requires a careful balancing of security needs with ethical concerns. By fostering open dialogue, promoting transparency and accountability, and establishing robust regulatory frameworks, we can harness the potential of olfactory surveillance technologies while safeguarding human rights, privacy, and the common good.

Chapter Eight: Smelling Disease: Stigma, Discrimination, and the Ethics of Olfactory Diagnosis

The human body, in its intricate workings, produces a symphony of smells. While some of these scents are considered socially acceptable, even desirable, others carry with them a heavy burden of stigma and fear, particularly when associated with illness and disease. This chapter explores the complex relationship between smell and disease, examining how olfactory cues have been used to diagnose illness, the social and ethical implications of associating certain smells with disease, and the challenges of navigating a world where the smell of sickness can lead to discrimination and social isolation.

The Nose as a Diagnostic Tool: A History of Olfactory Medicine:

The use of smell to diagnose illness has a long and fascinating history. Ancient physicians, from Hippocrates to Galen, believed that the body's odors could provide valuable clues about a patient's health. They developed elaborate systems of olfactory diagnosis, associating specific smells with different diseases. For example, a sweet, fruity odor on the breath was thought to indicate diabetes, while a foul-smelling urine was associated with bladder infections.

While some of these olfactory associations were based on keen observation and clinical experience, others were rooted in superstition and folklore. The miasma theory, which held that diseases were caused by bad air, led to the belief that certain smells, particularly those associated with decay and putrefaction, could transmit illness. This fear of contagion through smell contributed to the stigmatization of individuals with certain diseases, particularly those with infectious diseases like leprosy and the plague.

Despite the decline of the miasma theory in the 19th century with the advent of germ theory, the use of smell in medical diagnosis persisted. Physicians continued to rely on their olfactory senses to detect signs of illness, particularly in cases where other diagnostic tools were unavailable or unreliable. The smell of acetone on the breath, for example, can be a sign of diabetic ketoacidosis, a life-threatening complication of diabetes. The characteristic odor of a Pseudomonas aeruginosa infection, often described as grape-like or fruity, can help clinicians identify this opportunistic pathogen in patients with compromised immune systems.

Even today, in the age of advanced medical technology, the sense of smell can still play a role in diagnosis. Experienced clinicians may be able to detect subtle olfactory cues that suggest a particular illness, even before other symptoms become apparent. The smell of a patient's sweat, urine, or breath can provide valuable information about their metabolic state, the presence of infection, or even the onset of certain cancers.

The Stigma of Sickness: Olfactory Discrimination and Social Exclusion:

The association of certain smells with disease can have profound social and psychological consequences for individuals affected by these illnesses. The stigma of sickness, the negative social attitudes and beliefs associated with illness, can lead to discrimination, social isolation, and a diminished quality of life.

Individuals with illnesses that produce noticeable odors, such as fecal incontinence, colostomy bags, or certain skin conditions, may face significant challenges in their social interactions. They may be ostracized, avoided, or ridiculed because of their perceived smell. This can lead to feelings of shame, embarrassment, and a reluctance to engage in social activities.

The stigma of sickness can also affect access to employment, housing, and other essential services. Individuals with illnesses that produce noticeable odors may be denied employment opportunities or housing because of their perceived smell. This can perpetuate a cycle of poverty and social exclusion.

The stigma of sickness is not limited to illnesses that produce noticeable odors. Individuals with mental illnesses, for example, may also face olfactory discrimination. The smell of certain medications, such as antipsychotics, can be perceived as unpleasant or "chemical" by some individuals. This can lead to negative judgments about the individual's character or mental state, further contributing to the stigma associated with mental illness.

The Ethics of Olfactory Diagnosis: Balancing Benefits and Risks:

The use of smell in medical diagnosis raises a number of ethical considerations. While olfactory cues can provide valuable information about a patient's health, there are also risks associated with relying on smell as a diagnostic tool.

One of the main ethical challenges is the potential for misdiagnosis. The human olfactory system is highly subjective, and the perception of smell can be influenced by a variety of factors, including individual sensitivities, cultural backgrounds, and even emotional states. This can lead to misinterpretations of olfactory cues and inaccurate diagnoses.

The reliance on smell in diagnosis can also perpetuate the stigma of sickness. Associating certain smells with disease can reinforce negative stereotypes and contribute to the social isolation of individuals with these illnesses. This can have a detrimental impact on their psychological well-being and their ability to access healthcare and other essential services.

The use of olfactory diagnosis also raises privacy concerns. The smells emanating from our bodies can reveal a wealth of information about our health, diet, and even our genetic predispositions. The collection and analysis of olfactory data, particularly without informed consent, could lead to a new form of medical surveillance, potentially revealing intimate details about our lives without our knowledge or control.

The ethical use of olfactory diagnosis requires a careful balancing of the potential benefits and risks. Clinicians should be aware of the limitations of olfactory diagnosis and the potential for misinterpretation. They should also be sensitive to the social and psychological implications of associating certain smells with disease. The collection and use of olfactory data should be guided by ethical principles of informed consent, privacy, and confidentiality.

The Social Construction of Smell and Disease:

The association of certain smells with disease is not solely based on objective scientific evidence. It is also influenced by cultural norms, social values, and historical context. What one culture considers to be a "sickly" smell, another culture may find to be acceptable or even desirable.

For example, in some cultures, the smell of sweat is considered to be a sign of masculinity and virility. In other cultures, however, the smell of sweat is associated with poor hygiene and lack of social refinement. Similarly, the smell of certain foods, such as fermented fish sauce or aged cheese, may be considered a delicacy in some cultures but may be perceived as offensive or repulsive in others.

The social construction of smell and disease can have a profound impact on how individuals with certain illnesses are perceived and treated. For example, in some cultures, individuals with leprosy were historically ostracized and forced to live in isolated colonies because of the perceived smell of their disease. This social exclusion was based on the belief that the smell of leprosy could transmit the disease, even though this belief was not supported by scientific evidence.

The social construction of smell and disease can also influence the development and implementation of public health policies. In the

52

19th century, the fear of contagion through smell led to the implementation of sanitation policies that often targeted the living conditions of the poor and marginalized. These policies, while ostensibly aimed at eliminating disease, also served to reinforce social hierarchies and maintain order in a rapidly changing urban landscape.

Challenging Olfactory Stigma: Promoting Understanding and Empathy:

Challenging the stigma associated with the smell of disease requires a multi-faceted approach that addresses both the individual and societal levels. At the individual level, it is important to promote empathy and understanding for individuals with illnesses that produce noticeable odors. Educating the public about the causes and consequences of these illnesses can help to reduce fear and prejudice.

Open communication and dialogue can also play a role in challenging olfactory stigma. Individuals with illnesses that produce noticeable odors may benefit from discussing their experiences with others, sharing their challenges and coping strategies. This can help to reduce feelings of shame and isolation and promote a sense of shared humanity.

At the societal level, it is important to address the systemic factors that contribute to olfactory discrimination. This includes promoting access to healthcare and other essential services for individuals with illnesses that produce noticeable odors, challenging discriminatory practices in employment and housing, and advocating for policies that protect the rights and dignity of all individuals, regardless of their perceived smell.

The media can also play a role in challenging olfactory stigma. By portraying individuals with illnesses that produce noticeable odors in a positive and respectful light, the media can help to break down negative stereotypes and promote greater understanding and acceptance.

The Role of Technology in Mitigating Olfactory Stigma:

Advances in technology are providing new tools for mitigating the olfactory stigma associated with certain illnesses. These technologies can be broadly categorized into two main approaches:

- **Odor control technologies:** These technologies aim to reduce or eliminate the odors associated with certain illnesses. This can involve the use of absorbent materials, odor neutralizers, or even surgical interventions to address the underlying cause of the odor.

- **Assistive technologies:** These technologies aim to help individuals with illnesses that produce noticeable odors manage their condition and reduce the social impact of their smell. This can include devices that provide real-time feedback on odor levels, wearable devices that release fragrances to mask odors, or even smartphone apps that connect individuals with support groups and resources.

The development and use of these technologies raise ethical considerations about access, affordability, and the potential for unintended consequences. It is important to ensure that these technologies are available to all who need them, regardless of their socioeconomic status or geographical location. The potential impact of these technologies on individual autonomy and social interactions should also be carefully considered.

The Future of Smell and Disease: Towards a More Inclusive and Empathetic Smellscape:

The relationship between smell and disease is a complex and evolving one. As our understanding of the human olfactory system deepens, and as new technologies emerge to address the challenges of olfactory stigma, we have an opportunity to create a more inclusive and empathetic smellscape.

This requires a shift in our attitudes towards smell and disease. We must move away from a hierarchical view of smell, where certain smells are associated with health and purity while others are stigmatized and marginalized. Instead, we must embrace a more nuanced and compassionate understanding of the human body and its olfactory expressions.

Promoting olfactory literacy, the ability to identify, understand, and appreciate a diverse range of smells, can play a crucial role in this shift. Educating people about the biological, social, and cultural significance of smell can help to break down olfactory stereotypes and foster a greater appreciation for the diversity of human experience.

The development of ethical guidelines for the use of olfactory diagnosis and the collection and use of olfactory data is also essential. These guidelines should be grounded in principles of informed consent, privacy, and respect for human dignity.

Ultimately, creating a more inclusive and empathetic smellscape requires a collective effort. Researchers, clinicians, policymakers, educators, and individuals all have a role to play in challenging olfactory stigma, promoting understanding, and fostering a society where all individuals are valued and respected, regardless of their perceived smell.

Chapter Nine: The Odor of Otherness: Xenophobia, Racism, and the Olfactory Construction of Identity

Smell, an invisible yet potent force, has been instrumental in shaping perceptions of identity and difference throughout history. The human olfactory system, with its intricate ability to detect and interpret a vast array of scents, has often been employed to categorize individuals and groups, creating olfactory boundaries that reinforce social hierarchies and perpetuate prejudice. This chapter delves into the complex relationship between smell, xenophobia, and racism, exploring how olfactory perceptions have been used to construct notions of "otherness," justify discrimination, and shape the social and political landscape.

The Smell of the "Other": Olfactory Stereotypes and the Construction of Difference:

The human tendency to categorize and classify individuals and groups is deeply rooted in our evolutionary history. Our ability to quickly assess potential threats and allies has been crucial for survival. However, this innate tendency to categorize can also lead to the development of stereotypes and prejudices, particularly when applied to individuals or groups perceived as different or "other."

Smell, with its immediate and visceral impact on our senses, has often been employed as a marker of difference, a way of distinguishing "us" from "them." Olfactory stereotypes, generalizations about the smells associated with particular groups, have been used to reinforce social hierarchies, justify discrimination, and perpetuate prejudice.

Throughout history, certain ethnic and racial groups have been stereotyped based on their perceived smell. These olfactory stereotypes are often rooted in cultural biases, historical prejudices, and power dynamics. The association of certain smells with particular groups can lead to the dehumanization of these groups, portraying them as less civilized, less intelligent, or even less human.

Olfactory Xenophobia: The Fear of Foreign Smells:

Xenophobia, the fear or hatred of foreigners or strangers, often manifests as a fear or aversion to unfamiliar smells. The smells associated with different cultures, cuisines, and hygiene practices can be perceived as threatening or repulsive by those unfamiliar with them. This olfactory xenophobia can contribute to social exclusion, discrimination, and even violence against individuals or groups perceived as "foreign."

The history of immigration is replete with examples of olfactory xenophobia. In the 19th century, for example, Irish immigrants to the United States were often stereotyped as "dirty" and "smelly" by the dominant Anglo-Saxon population. This olfactory stereotype was used to justify discrimination in housing, employment, and social interactions.

Similar olfactory stereotypes have been applied to other immigrant groups throughout history, including Italians, Jews, Chinese, and Mexicans. These stereotypes often reflect a fear of the unknown, a discomfort with difference, and a desire to maintain social boundaries.

Olfactory Racism: The Smell of Skin Color and the Justification of Discrimination:

Olfactory racism, a particularly insidious form of prejudice, involves the association of certain smells with skin color or racial background. This can manifest as the belief that individuals of a particular race have a distinct and unpleasant body odor. This belief, often rooted in historical prejudices and pseudoscientific theories, has been used to justify discrimination, segregation, and even violence against racial minorities.

In the 19th century, for example, some scientists and social theorists claimed that individuals of African descent had a distinct and unpleasant body odor that was evidence of their supposed inferiority. This olfactory stereotype was used to justify slavery, segregation, and the denial of basic human rights to African Americans.

Similar olfactory stereotypes have been applied to other racial groups, including indigenous populations, Asian Americans, and Latino/a/x individuals. These stereotypes are often rooted in a desire to maintain racial hierarchies and justify social inequalities.

The Smell of "Hygiene" and the Policing of Bodies:

The concept of "hygiene" and its associated smells have also been used to reinforce social hierarchies and exert social control. In the 19th century, the rise of the public health movement and the growing emphasis on personal hygiene led to the association of cleanliness with morality and social respectability. The use of soap, deodorant, and other hygiene products became a marker of social status and a means of distinguishing oneself from the "unclean" and "uncivilized" lower classes.

This association of cleanliness with morality and social status has often been used to justify the policing of bodies, particularly the bodies of marginalized groups. For example, in the 19th and early 20th centuries, indigenous populations in North America were often forced to attend boarding schools where they were subjected to strict hygiene regimens and forced to abandon their traditional practices. This was often justified as a way of "civilizing" these populations and assimilating them into the dominant culture.

Similar hygiene practices have been used to control and regulate the bodies of other marginalized groups, including immigrants, racial minorities, and individuals with disabilities. The emphasis on cleanliness and its associated smells can be a way of enforcing social norms, reinforcing power dynamics, and perpetuating discrimination.

Olfactory Microaggressions: The Subtle Assault of Smell-Based Prejudice:

Olfactory microaggressions, subtle and often unintentional acts of smell-based prejudice, can have a significant impact on the well-being and social experiences of individuals from marginalized groups. These microaggressions can manifest in various forms, including:

- **Comments about body odor:** Making comments about an individual's body odor, particularly if it is perceived as "different" or "unpleasant," can be a form of olfactory microaggression.

- **Negative reactions to food smells:** Expressing disgust or aversion to the smells of certain foods, particularly foods associated with specific cultures or ethnic groups, can be a form of olfactory microaggression.

- **Assumptions about hygiene practices:** Making assumptions about an individual's hygiene practices based on their perceived smell can be a form of olfactory microaggression.

- **Use of air fresheners or perfumes to mask smells:** The excessive use of air fresheners or perfumes to mask smells associated with certain individuals or groups can be a form of olfactory microaggression, suggesting that their natural smells are unacceptable.

Olfactory microaggressions, while often unintentional, can contribute to feelings of alienation, shame, and social isolation among individuals from marginalized groups. They can also reinforce negative stereotypes and perpetuate discrimination.

Challenging Olfactory Prejudice: Promoting Olfactory Literacy and Empathy:

Challenging olfactory prejudice requires a multi-faceted approach that addresses both the individual and societal levels. At the individual level, it is important to promote olfactory literacy, the ability to identify, understand, and appreciate a diverse range of smells. This includes educating people about the cultural and historical significance of smell, challenging olfactory stereotypes, and fostering a greater appreciation for the diversity of human olfactory experiences.

Empathy and perspective-taking are also crucial in challenging olfactory prejudice. Recognizing that our olfactory perceptions are shaped by our own cultural backgrounds and personal experiences can help us to understand and appreciate the olfactory preferences of others.

At the societal level, it is important to address the systemic factors that contribute to olfactory discrimination. This includes challenging discriminatory practices in housing, employment, and social interactions. It also involves promoting diversity and inclusivity in the media, education, and other social institutions.

Policy interventions can also play a role in challenging olfactory prejudice. For example, anti-discrimination laws can be expanded to include protection against olfactory discrimination. Public awareness campaigns can be launched to educate people about the harmful effects of olfactory prejudice and promote greater understanding and tolerance.

The Power of Smell in Shaping Identity and Belonging:

While smell has often been used to create and reinforce social divisions, it can also be a source of identity, community, and belonging. The smells associated with our homes, our families, our cultures, and our traditions can evoke powerful emotions and memories, creating a sense of connection and shared identity.

For immigrant communities, the smells of their traditional foods and spices can be a reminder of their homeland and a source of comfort and connection in a new environment. For religious communities, the smells of incense, candles, or other ritual objects can create a sense of sacred space and shared spiritual identity.

Recognizing the positive and affirming aspects of smell can help to counter the negative and divisive uses of smell in perpetuating prejudice and discrimination. By embracing the diversity of human olfactory experiences and celebrating the unique smellscapes of different cultures and communities, we can create a more inclusive and harmonious world.

The Future of Smell and Identity: Towards an Olfactory Ethos of Respect and Understanding:

As our understanding of the human olfactory system deepens, and as we become more aware of the profound impact of smell on our social interactions and perceptions of identity, it is essential to develop an olfactory ethos of respect and understanding. This ethos should be grounded in the recognition that our olfactory preferences are shaped by our individual experiences, cultural backgrounds, and social contexts.

It should also be guided by the principles of empathy, tolerance, and inclusivity. We must learn to appreciate the diversity of human olfactory experiences and to challenge the use of smell to create and reinforce social divisions.

The future of smell and identity requires a conscious effort to move beyond olfactory stereotypes and prejudices. By promoting olfactory literacy, fostering empathy, and challenging discrimination, we can create a world where smell is a source of connection, understanding, and shared humanity.

Chapter Ten: Perfumed Bodies: Gender, Sexuality, and the Ethics of Olfactory Self-Fashioning

The human body is a canvas for self-expression, and smell, often an overlooked element of our personal presentation, plays a significant role in how we construct and communicate our identities. This chapter explores the intricate relationship between smell, gender, and sexuality, examining how olfactory cues are used to create and reinforce gender norms, express sexual desires, and challenge traditional notions of identity. We will delve into the ethics of olfactory self-fashioning, the ways in which we use scents to shape our personal and social identities, and the implications of these choices for individual autonomy, social justice, and the politics of smell.

The Gendered Smellscape: Olfactory Stereotypes and the Construction of Masculinity and Femininity:

From the moment we are born, we are immersed in a world of gendered smells. Baby girls are often swaddled in pink blankets and bathed in floral-scented lotions, while baby boys are wrapped in blue and doused in powdery or musky fragrances. These early olfactory experiences contribute to the construction of gendered identities, associating certain smells with femininity and others with masculinity.

This gendered smellscape continues throughout our lives. Women are often encouraged to cultivate a "feminine" scent, associated with floral, fruity, or sweet fragrances, while men are expected to exude a "masculine" smell, characterized by woody, musky, or spicy notes. These olfactory stereotypes are reinforced through advertising, media representations, and social interactions.

The fragrance industry plays a significant role in perpetuating these gendered smellscapes. Perfumes and colognes are often marketed with distinct gendered identities, using language, imagery, and even bottle designs to appeal to specific gender roles and expectations. Women's fragrances are often advertised as "romantic," "sensual," or "elegant," while men's fragrances are promoted as "powerful," "confident," or "adventurous."

These gendered marketing strategies can reinforce narrow and limiting notions of masculinity and femininity. They can also contribute to olfactory insecurity among individuals who do not conform to these stereotypes, leading to pressure to acquire the "right" scents to fit in and be accepted.

The Smell of Seduction: Fragrance and the Performance of Sexuality:

Smell has long been associated with sexuality and seduction. Throughout history, perfumes and other scented products have been used to enhance attractiveness, arouse desire, and communicate sexual availability. The ancient Egyptians, for example, used perfumes made from flowers, spices, and resins to adorn their bodies and attract potential mates.

In many cultures, certain smells are believed to have aphrodisiac properties, enhancing sexual desire and arousal. For example, the scent of jasmine is often associated with sensuality and romance, while the smell of musk is believed to have a stimulating effect on the libido.

The fragrance industry often capitalizes on these associations, marketing perfumes and colognes as tools for seduction and sexual conquest. Advertisements often feature suggestive imagery and language, implying that the use of a particular fragrance can enhance one's sexual allure and lead to romantic or sexual success.

However, the association of fragrance with sexuality can also be problematic. It can contribute to the objectification of bodies, reducing individuals to their perceived sexual attractiveness based solely on their scent. It can also reinforce harmful stereotypes about gender and sexuality, suggesting that women should be passive objects of desire while men should be active pursuers.

Challenging Olfactory Gender Norms: The Rise of Gender-Neutral and Inclusive Fragrances:

In recent years, there has been a growing movement to challenge traditional olfactory gender norms. This has led to the rise of gender-neutral fragrances, designed to appeal to individuals of all genders, and inclusive fragrance brands that celebrate the diversity of human olfactory experiences.

Gender-neutral fragrances often feature notes that are not traditionally associated with either masculinity or femininity, such as citrus, green tea, or fig. These fragrances are marketed as a way of expressing individuality and breaking free from restrictive gender stereotypes.

Inclusive fragrance brands are also challenging the traditional binary approach to fragrance marketing. These brands often feature a diverse range of scents, designed to appeal to a wide range of tastes and preferences. They also often use inclusive language and imagery in their marketing campaigns, celebrating the beauty and diversity of all genders and sexual orientations.

The rise of gender-neutral and inclusive fragrances reflects a broader shift in societal attitudes towards gender and sexuality. As gender roles become more fluid and less rigid, individuals are increasingly seeking ways to express their identities through scent that go beyond traditional binary categories.

The Ethics of Olfactory Self-Fashioning: Agency, Authenticity, and Social Responsibility:

The use of fragrance to shape our personal and social identities raises ethical questions about individual agency, authenticity, and social responsibility. Olfactory self-fashioning, the conscious and deliberate use of scent to construct and communicate our identities, can be a powerful tool for self-expression and empowerment.

However, it is important to be mindful of the potential impact of our olfactory choices on others. The scents we choose to wear can affect the people around us, triggering allergies, sensitivities, or even negative emotions. It is important to be respectful of others' olfactory preferences and to avoid imposing our own scent choices on them.

The ethics of olfactory self-fashioning also involves considerations of authenticity. The fragrance industry often promotes the idea that certain scents can transform our identities, making us more attractive, confident, or successful. However, it is important to be critical of these marketing claims and to be mindful of the potential for inauthenticity in our olfactory choices.

Authentic olfactory self-fashioning involves choosing scents that reflect our true selves, rather than trying to conform to external expectations or idealized images. It also involves being mindful of the social and cultural meanings associated with different scents and avoiding the appropriation or misrepresentation of these meanings.

The Politics of Smell and the Olfactory Construction of Identity:

The use of smell to construct and communicate identity is not just a matter of personal preference; it is also deeply intertwined with the politics of smell. The ways in which we perceive and interpret smells are shaped by cultural norms, social hierarchies, and power dynamics.

For example, the association of certain smells with poverty or lower social classes can lead to olfactory discrimination, where individuals are judged and treated differently based solely on their perceived smell. This can have a significant impact on their access to employment, housing, and other essential services.

The use of smell to construct notions of "otherness" can also have political implications. The association of certain smells with particular ethnic or racial groups can contribute to xenophobia and racism, justifying discrimination and even violence against these groups.

The politics of smell also extends to the regulation of smells in public spaces. The enforcement of olfactory norms, such as restrictions on smoking or the use of strong perfumes, can be a way of exerting social control and maintaining order. However, these regulations can also be discriminatory, targeting certain groups or practices while privileging others.

Olfactory Inclusivity: Creating a More Just and Equitable Smellscape:

Promoting olfactory inclusivity requires challenging olfactory stereotypes, dismantling olfactory hierarchies, and creating a more just and equitable smellscape. This involves recognizing the diversity of human olfactory experiences and respecting the right of individuals to express their identities through scent without fear of judgment or discrimination.

Educating people about the cultural and historical significance of smell can help to promote greater understanding and appreciation for the diversity of human olfactory practices. Challenging olfactory stereotypes and microaggressions can also help to create a more inclusive and welcoming environment for all.

Policy interventions can also play a role in promoting olfactory inclusivity. For example, anti-discrimination laws can be expanded to include protection against olfactory discrimination. Public awareness campaigns can be launched to educate people about the harmful effects of olfactory prejudice and promote greater understanding and tolerance.

The fragrance industry also has a role to play in promoting olfactory inclusivity. By developing and marketing gender-neutral and inclusive fragrances, the industry can challenge traditional olfactory gender norms and celebrate the diversity of human olfactory experiences.

Creating a more just and equitable smellscape requires a collective effort. By promoting olfactory literacy, challenging discrimination, and embracing the diversity of human olfactory experiences, we can create a world where smell is a source of connection, understanding, and shared humanity.

Chapter Eleven: The Smell of History: Memory, Nostalgia, and the Ethics of Olfactory Heritage

Smell possesses a remarkable ability to unlock memories, transporting us back to specific moments in our past with a vividness that other senses often fail to achieve. A whiff of freshly baked bread might evoke childhood memories of a grandparent's kitchen, the scent of a particular perfume might conjure up a long-lost love, or the smell of rain on dry pavement might trigger a wave of nostalgia for a simpler time. This chapter explores the intricate relationship between smell, memory, and nostalgia, examining how olfactory cues shape our understanding of the past, the ethical considerations that arise when manipulating olfactory memories, and the potential for smell to be used to preserve and transmit cultural heritage.

The Proust Phenomenon: Olfactory-Evoked Autobiographical Memories:

The phenomenon of olfactory-evoked autobiographical memories, often referred to as the "Proust phenomenon" after the French novelist Marcel Proust, highlights the unique power of smell to trigger vivid and emotionally charged recollections of past experiences. Proust, in his epic novel "In Search of Lost Time," famously described how the taste and smell of a madeleine cake dipped in tea triggered a flood of memories from his childhood, transporting him back to a specific moment in his past with remarkable clarity.

These olfactory-triggered memories, also known as "Proustian memories," are often more intense and emotionally charged than memories evoked by other senses. This is likely due to the direct connection between the olfactory system and the amygdala, the brain region responsible for processing emotions, and the hippocampus, the region involved in memory formation.

The smells that trigger Proustian memories are often highly personal and idiosyncratic, linked to specific events, individuals, or places in our past. For example, the smell of freshly cut grass might evoke memories of childhood summers spent playing outdoors, while the smell of a particular spice might trigger recollections of a favorite family meal.

These olfactory memories can be both positive and negative. The smell of a hospital might evoke memories of a difficult illness or the loss of a loved one, while the smell of a campfire might trigger recollections of happy times spent with friends and family.

The Neuroscience of Olfactory Memory:

The unique power of smell to evoke memories is rooted in the neuroanatomy of the olfactory system. Unlike our other senses, which are routed through the thalamus, a sensory relay center in the brain, before reaching the cortex, smell has a direct pathway to the amygdala and the hippocampus.

The amygdala plays a crucial role in processing emotions, particularly fear and pleasure. This direct connection between the olfactory system and the amygdala explains why certain smells can evoke strong emotional responses, such as the fear triggered by the smell of smoke or the pleasure elicited by the smell of a favorite food.

The hippocampus is involved in the formation and retrieval of memories. The direct connection between the olfactory system and the hippocampus allows smells to be strongly associated with specific events and experiences, creating lasting olfactory memories.

The olfactory system also has connections to other brain regions involved in memory and emotion, such as the orbitofrontal cortex, which is involved in decision-making and assigning value to sensory experiences, and the insula, which is involved in processing bodily sensations and emotional awareness.

These intricate neural connections explain why olfactory memories are often so vivid, emotionally charged, and resistant to forgetting.

Nostalgia: The Smell of Longing for the Past:

Nostalgia, a sentimental longing or wistful affection for the past, is often triggered by olfactory cues. The smells associated with our childhood, our homes, our cultures, and our traditions can evoke a powerful sense of nostalgia, transporting us back to a time that is perceived as simpler, happier, or more meaningful.

The smells of holidays, such as the scent of pine needles at Christmas or the aroma of pumpkin pie at Thanksgiving, can trigger nostalgic memories of family gatherings and festive celebrations. The smells of familiar places, such as the scent of the ocean at a childhood vacation spot or the aroma of freshly brewed coffee at a favorite cafe, can evoke a sense of longing for a time and place that is no longer accessible.

Nostalgia can be a powerful and complex emotion. It can provide a sense of comfort, connection, and continuity with the past. It can also be a source of sadness, regret, or even a romanticized view of the past that ignores its complexities and challenges.

The Ethics of Manipulating Olfactory Memories:

The ability to manipulate olfactory memories raises ethical questions about the authenticity of our recollections and the potential for these memories to be used for manipulative purposes. Advances in technology, such as virtual reality and olfactory displays, are creating new possibilities for recreating past smellscapes and evoking specific olfactory memories.

While these technologies have the potential to enhance our understanding of the past and provide therapeutic benefits for individuals with memory loss or trauma, they also raise concerns about the potential for these memories to be altered or fabricated.

The ethical use of olfactory memory manipulation requires careful consideration of the potential benefits and risks. It is essential to ensure that these technologies are used in a transparent and responsible manner, with informed consent from individuals whose memories are being manipulated.

The Smell of History: Olfactory Heritage and the Preservation of the Past:

Smell can play a crucial role in preserving and transmitting cultural heritage. The smells associated with historical events, places, and traditions can provide a unique and visceral connection to the past, allowing us to experience history in a more immersive and engaging way.

For example, the smell of gunpowder might evoke the sights and sounds of a battlefield, the scent of incense might transport us to a medieval cathedral, or the aroma of freshly baked bread might give us a glimpse into the daily lives of people in a bygone era.

Olfactory heritage, the preservation and transmission of historically significant smells, is an emerging field that seeks to capture and recreate the smellscapes of the past. This can involve the collection and analysis of historical scents, the development of olfactory displays and exhibits, and the integration of smell into historical narratives and interpretations.

The preservation of olfactory heritage can provide valuable insights into the past, enriching our understanding of history and culture. It can also create opportunities for empathy and connection with past generations, fostering a deeper appreciation for our shared human experience.

Olfactory Archives: Preserving the Smells of the Past for Future Generations:

The creation of olfactory archives, collections of historically significant smells, is an important step in preserving olfactory heritage. These archives can be used for research, education, and even the recreation of past smellscapes for future generations.

The collection and preservation of historical scents can be a challenging task. Smell is a fleeting and ephemeral phenomenon, and the chemical compounds that create smells can be difficult to capture and preserve over time.

However, advances in technology are providing new tools for olfactory archiving. For example, headspace technology, which involves capturing and analyzing the volatile compounds that create smells, can be used to create a digital "fingerprint" of a particular scent. This fingerprint can then be used to recreate the smell using olfactory displays or other technologies.

Olfactory archives can also include historical artifacts that retain their original scents, such as clothing, furniture, or even documents. These artifacts can provide a direct connection to the past, allowing us to experience the smells of a bygone era.

The Ethics of Olfactory Heritage: Authenticity, Representation, and Access:

The preservation and presentation of olfactory heritage raise ethical questions about authenticity, representation, and access. It is essential to ensure that the smellscapes of the past are recreated in a way that is accurate, respectful, and accessible to all.

The authenticity of olfactory heritage can be challenging to establish, as historical records of smells are often incomplete or unreliable. The interpretation of historical scents can also be subjective, influenced by cultural biases and personal experiences.

The representation of olfactory heritage should be inclusive and diverse, reflecting the smellscapes of different cultures and communities. It is important to avoid perpetuating olfactory stereotypes or erasing the olfactory experiences of marginalized groups.

Access to olfactory heritage should be equitable, ensuring that all individuals have the opportunity to experience and learn from the smells of the past. This includes making olfactory displays and exhibits accessible to individuals with disabilities and providing translations and interpretations for diverse audiences.

Olfactory Tourism: Experiencing History Through Smell:

Olfactory tourism, a growing trend in the heritage and tourism industries, involves incorporating smell into historical sites, museums, and other cultural attractions. This can enhance the visitor experience, providing a more immersive and engaging connection to the past.

For example, historical sites might recreate the smells of daily life in a bygone era, such as the smells of cooking, farming, or craft production. Museums might use olfactory displays to evoke the smells associated with historical events, such as the smell of gunpowder on a battlefield or the scent of incense in a temple.

Olfactory tourism can also be used to promote cultural understanding and appreciation. By experiencing the smellscapes of different cultures and historical periods, visitors can gain a deeper understanding of the diversity of human olfactory experiences.

The Future of Smell and History: Towards an Olfactory-Rich Understanding of the Past:

The relationship between smell and history is a rich and complex one. As our understanding of the human olfactory system deepens, and as new technologies emerge for capturing, preserving, and recreating historical scents, we have an opportunity to develop a more olfactory-rich understanding of the past.

This involves integrating smell into historical narratives, interpretations, and educational programs. It also requires challenging traditional notions of history as a purely visual and textual experience, recognizing the importance of smell in shaping our understanding of the past.

The future of smell and history also requires a commitment to preserving olfactory heritage for future generations. The creation of olfactory archives, the development of ethical guidelines for olfactory memory manipulation, and the promotion of olfactory tourism can all contribute to a more nuanced and immersive experience of history.

By embracing the power of smell to unlock memories, evoke emotions, and connect us to the past, we can enrich our understanding of history, culture, and the human experience.

Chapter Twelve: Food and the Ethics of Smell: Cultural Practices, Culinary Traditions, and the Morality of Taste

The aroma of freshly baked bread, the pungent scent of spices wafting from a street vendor's cart, the comforting smell of a simmering stew – food and smell are inextricably intertwined. Our olfactory sense plays a crucial role in our experience of food, shaping our perceptions of flavor, influencing our dietary choices, and even triggering deep-seated emotional and cultural associations. This chapter explores the complex relationship between food and the ethics of smell, examining how olfactory cues are embedded in cultural practices and culinary traditions, the moral judgments we make about food based on its smell, and the ethical considerations that arise in a world where food production and consumption are increasingly globalized and industrialized.

The Olfactory Symphony of Flavor: How Smell Shapes Our Perception of Taste:

Our perception of flavor is not solely determined by our taste buds; it is a multisensory experience in which smell plays a dominant role. When we eat, volatile molecules released from the food travel through the back of our nasal passages to the olfactory epithelium, where they interact with olfactory receptors, triggering a cascade of neural signals that are interpreted by the brain as smell. This olfactory information combines with the signals from our taste buds, which detect basic tastes like sweet, sour, salty, bitter, and umami, to create the complex and nuanced experience we perceive as flavor.

The contribution of smell to flavor is particularly evident when we have a stuffy nose. When our sense of smell is impaired, food often tastes bland and unappealing, highlighting the crucial role that olfaction plays in our enjoyment of food. Studies have shown that individuals with anosmia, the loss of the sense of smell, often experience a significant decrease in their quality of life, as they lose the ability to fully appreciate the flavors of food and the olfactory nuances of their environment.

The interplay between smell and taste is not a simple one-to-one relationship. The same basic taste can be perceived differently depending on the accompanying smell. For example, a sweet taste paired with a fruity smell might be perceived as a strawberry flavor, while the same sweet taste paired with a chocolatey smell might be interpreted as a chocolate flavor.

This complex interplay between smell and taste allows for an incredible diversity of flavors in the culinary world. Chefs and food artisans skillfully combine different ingredients and cooking techniques to create dishes that stimulate our olfactory senses and tantalize our taste buds.

The Smell of Culture: Olfactory Traditions and Culinary Identity:

Food and smell are deeply embedded in cultural practices and culinary traditions. The smells associated with different cuisines can evoke a sense of place, identity, and belonging. For example, the aroma of curry spices might transport us to the bustling streets of India, the scent of garlic and olive oil might evoke memories of a family meal in Italy, or the smell of smoky barbecue might conjure up images of a backyard cookout in the American South.

These olfactory associations are not just arbitrary; they are often rooted in the history, geography, and cultural values of a particular region or community. The spices used in Indian cuisine, for example, reflect the country's rich history of trade and cultural exchange with other parts of Asia and the Middle East. The abundance of garlic and olive oil in Italian cuisine is a testament to the country's Mediterranean climate and agricultural traditions.

Food and smell can also play a role in cultural rituals and celebrations. For example, the smell of incense might be associated with religious ceremonies in some cultures, while the aroma of freshly baked bread might be a symbol of hospitality and welcome in others.

The globalization of food and culture has led to the exchange and fusion of culinary traditions, creating new and exciting olfactory experiences. However, it is important to be mindful of the potential for cultural appropriation and the erasure of traditional foodways. When adopting or adapting culinary traditions from other cultures, it is essential to do so with respect and understanding, acknowledging the cultural significance of food and smell in the original context.

The Morality of Taste: Olfactory Judgments and Food Ethics:

Our olfactory perceptions of food are not just about pleasure and enjoyment; they are also imbued with moral judgments and ethical considerations. The smells we associate with food can influence our dietary choices, shaping our perceptions of what is considered edible, desirable, or even morally acceptable.

For example, in many Western cultures, the smell of meat is often associated with strength, virility, and even social status. Conversely, the smell of vegetables might be perceived as bland, unappetizing, or even indicative of poverty or lower social class. These olfactory associations can contribute to unhealthy dietary choices, promoting the consumption of meat over vegetables.

The smell of food can also trigger disgust reactions, particularly when associated with decay, spoilage, or contamination. This disgust response is an evolutionary adaptation that helps us to avoid consuming foods that might be harmful or contaminated. However, disgust reactions can also be culturally conditioned, varying across different societies and even within the same society.

For example, the smell of fermented foods, such as cheese or fish sauce, might be considered a delicacy in some cultures but might elicit a strong disgust response in others. The smell of insects, which are a source of protein in many parts of the world, might be considered repulsive by individuals who have not been exposed to this food source.

The moral judgments we make about food based on its smell can have ethical implications. For example, the aversion to the smell of certain foods can contribute to food waste, as perfectly edible foods are discarded because of their perceived smell. The stigmatization of certain foods based on their smell can also lead to discrimination against cultural groups whose culinary traditions incorporate these foods.

The Ethics of Food Production: Olfactory Impacts and Environmental Justice:

The industrialization of food production has had a significant impact on the olfactory environment, both in rural areas and urban centers. Large-scale animal farms, also known as Concentrated Animal Feeding Operations (CAFOs), are a major source of air pollution and noxious smells. These farms confine thousands of animals in close quarters, producing vast quantities of manure and other waste products that release strong and pervasive odors into the surrounding environment.

The smell of CAFOs, often described as overpowering, nauseating, and ammonia-like, can travel for miles, affecting the quality of life of nearby residents. Studies have shown that exposure to CAFO odors is associated with a range of health problems, including respiratory illnesses, headaches, nausea, and stress.

CAFOs are disproportionately located in or near communities of color and low-income communities. This siting pattern reflects a history of racial discrimination and economic inequality in the agricultural industry. The residents of these communities have often been denied the opportunity to participate in decision-making processes regarding the location of CAFOs, and they have borne the brunt of the negative environmental impacts of these facilities, including exposure to noxious smells.

The ethics of food production require a careful consideration of the olfactory impacts of different farming practices and the distribution of these impacts across different communities. Environmental justice principles call for a more equitable distribution of environmental burdens and benefits, ensuring that marginalized communities are not disproportionately exposed to pollution and other environmental hazards, including noxious smells.

The Smell of Sustainability: Olfactory Considerations in Food Choices:

The growing awareness of the environmental and social impacts of food production has led to an increasing interest in sustainable food systems. Sustainable food systems aim to produce food in a way that is environmentally sound, socially just, and economically viable.

Olfactory considerations can play a role in promoting sustainable food choices. For example, choosing locally sourced foods can reduce the environmental impact of transportation, which can also reduce the exposure to noxious smells associated with long-distance trucking of food products. Choosing plant-based foods over meat can also reduce the environmental impact of agriculture, as livestock production is a major contributor to greenhouse gas emissions and other environmental problems, including the production of noxious smells from CAFOs.

Supporting sustainable farming practices, such as organic agriculture and agroforestry, can also contribute to a more pleasant and healthy olfactory environment. These farming practices often involve the use of natural fertilizers and pest control methods, which can reduce the need for synthetic chemicals that can release harmful or unpleasant smells into the environment.

The Future of Food and Smell: Ethical Challenges and Opportunities in a Changing World:

The future of food and smell will be shaped by a confluence of factors, including technological advancements, demographic shifts, and changing cultural norms. Advances in biotechnology, for example, are creating new possibilities for manipulating the flavors and smells of food, raising ethical questions about the authenticity and safety of these engineered foods.

The growing global population and the increasing demand for food are putting pressure on existing food systems, leading to concerns about food security and the environmental sustainability of food production. The ethics of food production and consumption will become increasingly important as we navigate these challenges.

Climate change is also expected to have a significant impact on food production, affecting crop yields, livestock production, and the availability of water resources. The changing climate may also alter the smellscapes of different regions, as rising temperatures and changing precipitation patterns affect the growth and distribution of plants and animals.

The globalization of food and culture continues to shape our olfactory experiences, creating new opportunities for culinary innovation and cultural exchange. However, it is important to be mindful of the potential for cultural appropriation and the erasure of traditional foodways.

The future of food and smell requires a careful consideration of the ethical implications of our choices. We must strive to create food systems that are environmentally sustainable, socially just, and culturally respectful. This involves promoting olfactory literacy, challenging olfactory stereotypes, and fostering a greater appreciation for the diversity of human olfactory experiences.

By embracing the power of smell to enhance our enjoyment of food, connect us to our cultural heritage, and guide us towards more sustainable and ethical food choices, we can create a more fragrant and flavorful future for all.

Chapter Thirteen: The Smell of Death: Mortuary Rituals, Grief, and the Ethics of Olfactory Commemoration

Death, an inevitable part of the human experience, carries with it a unique olfactory signature. The smell of decay, often perceived as repulsive and unsettling, has profound cultural and psychological significance, shaping our rituals surrounding death, our expressions of grief, and our efforts to commemorate the deceased. This chapter explores the complex relationship between smell and death, examining how olfactory cues are intertwined with mortuary practices, the role of smell in the grieving process, and the ethical considerations that arise when dealing with the smells of death in a world increasingly focused on sanitation and odor control.

The Olfactory Taboo: The Smell of Death and the Cultural Construction of Disgust:

The smell of death, often described as a pungent, sickly-sweet odor, is a powerful trigger for disgust reactions in many cultures. This aversion to the smell of decay is likely an evolutionary adaptation, serving as a warning signal to avoid potentially harmful or contaminated substances. However, the cultural construction of disgust surrounding the smell of death goes beyond this basic biological response.

In many societies, the smell of death is considered taboo, a source of pollution and impurity that must be avoided or masked. This olfactory taboo is often reflected in mortuary rituals, which aim to cleanse the body of the deceased, prepare it for burial or cremation, and minimize the presence of unpleasant odors.

For example, in many cultures, the body of the deceased is washed and perfumed before burial. This practice serves both a hygienic purpose and a symbolic one, cleansing the body of impurities and preparing it for its transition to the afterlife. The use of incense, flowers, and other fragrant substances in funeral rituals also serves to mask the smell of death and create a more pleasant olfactory environment for mourners.

The olfactory taboo surrounding death is also reflected in language. We often use euphemisms to avoid directly referencing the smell of decay, such as "passing away," "departed," or "resting in peace." This linguistic avoidance further reinforces the cultural aversion to the smell of death.

The Smell of Grief: Olfactory Cues and the Emotional Landscape of Mourning:

The smell of a loved one's body, even after death, can evoke powerful emotions and memories. The familiar scent of their perfume, their hair, or their clothing can trigger a flood of grief, reminding us of their absence and the finality of death.

For some individuals, the smell of death can be a source of comfort, a tangible reminder of the deceased's physical presence. For others, it can be a source of intense pain and distress, exacerbating the feelings of loss and grief.

The olfactory experiences of grief are often highly personal and idiosyncratic. Some individuals may find solace in the smell of the deceased's belongings, while others may find it too painful to bear. There is no right or wrong way to experience the smells of grief.

The cultural context in which grief is experienced can also shape olfactory perceptions. In some cultures, the public expression of grief is encouraged, and the smells of death are not necessarily masked or avoided. In other cultures, however, grief is often expressed more privately, and the smells of death are typically minimized or concealed.

Mortuary Rituals: Managing the Smells of Death Across Cultures:

Mortuary rituals, the ceremonies and practices surrounding death, vary widely across cultures. However, many of these rituals share a common goal: to manage the smells of death and prepare the body for its final disposition.

In some cultures, the body of the deceased is embalmed, a process that involves injecting chemicals into the body to preserve it and prevent decay. Embalming can significantly reduce the smell of death, allowing for a longer viewing period and facilitating transportation of the body over long distances.

In other cultures, the body of the deceased is buried or cremated shortly after death, minimizing the time that the body is exposed to the elements and reducing the likelihood of unpleasant odors.

The choice of burial or cremation can also be influenced by olfactory considerations. Cremation, for example, can eliminate the smell of death entirely, while burial can lead to the gradual release of decomposition odors into the surrounding environment.

The location of cemeteries and burial grounds can also be influenced by olfactory concerns. In many societies, cemeteries are located on the outskirts of towns or cities, away from residential areas, to minimize the potential for unpleasant smells to affect the living.

The Ethics of Embalming: Preservation, Deception, and the Right to a Natural Death:

Embalming, a common practice in many Western cultures, raises ethical questions about the manipulation of the body after death, the deception of mourners, and the right to a natural decomposition process.

Embalming involves the injection of formaldehyde and other chemicals into the body to preserve it and prevent decay. This process can significantly alter the appearance of the deceased, making them appear more lifelike than they would naturally.

Some critics argue that embalming is a form of deception, creating a false impression of the deceased and preventing mourners from fully confronting the reality of death. They also argue that embalming interferes with the natural decomposition process, preventing the body from returning to the earth in a timely and environmentally friendly manner.

Proponents of embalming argue that it provides a valuable service to mourners, allowing them to view the deceased in a more peaceful and dignified state. They also argue that embalming can prevent the spread of disease and facilitate the transportation of the body over long distances.

The ethics of embalming involve a balancing of competing values, including the desire to honor the deceased, the needs of mourners, and the right to a natural death. The decision of whether or not to embalm a body should be made on a case-by-case basis, taking into account the wishes of the deceased, the cultural context, and the potential environmental impacts.

The Smell of Death in the Digital Age: Virtual Memorials and Olfactory Representations:

The rise of the internet and digital technologies has created new ways of commemorating the deceased, including virtual memorials, online obituaries, and social media tributes. These digital platforms offer opportunities for sharing memories, expressing grief, and creating a sense of community among mourners.

However, the digital representation of death often lacks the olfactory dimension of traditional memorial practices. The smell of flowers at a funeral, the scent of incense at a memorial service, or the familiar smell of a loved one's belongings can evoke powerful emotions and memories that are difficult to replicate in the digital realm.

Some researchers and technologists are exploring the possibilities of incorporating smell into digital memorials, using olfactory displays or other technologies to recreate the smells associated with the deceased or the places and events that were meaningful to them.

These olfactory representations of death raise ethical questions about the authenticity of these digital smellscapes and the potential for these technologies to be used for manipulative or exploitative purposes.

The ethical use of olfactory technologies in digital memorials requires careful consideration of the potential benefits and risks. It is essential to ensure that these technologies are used in a transparent and responsible manner, with informed consent from the families of the deceased.

The Right to Smell Death: Challenging Olfactory Taboos and Embracing the Natural Decomposition Process:

In a world increasingly focused on sanitation and odor control, the smell of death has become even more taboo. The natural decomposition process, once an accepted part of the life cycle, is now often viewed as something to be avoided or concealed.

This aversion to the smell of death can have negative consequences for our relationship with mortality and our ability to grieve and heal after loss. The denial of death and the suppression of grief can lead to psychological distress and a diminished quality of life.

Some individuals and communities are challenging the olfactory taboo surrounding death, advocating for the right to smell death and embrace the natural decomposition process. They argue that experiencing the smells of death can be a cathartic and healing experience, allowing us to confront the reality of mortality and come to terms with our own grief.

The "death positive" movement, which promotes open and honest conversations about death and dying, has also embraced the natural decomposition process. This movement advocates for alternative burial practices, such as green burials, which allow the body to decompose naturally without the use of embalming fluids or other chemicals.

The right to smell death is not about celebrating or fetishizing death; it is about acknowledging the natural cycle of life and death and accepting the smells of decay as a part of that cycle. It is also about challenging the cultural taboos that have made death a topic to be avoided or whispered about.

Olfactory Commemoration: Using Smell to Honor the Dead and Preserve Memories:

Smell can be a powerful tool for commemorating the deceased and preserving their memories. The creation of olfactory memorials, spaces or objects that evoke the smells associated with the deceased, can provide a unique and tangible way of remembering and honoring loved ones.

Olfactory memorials can take many forms. For example, a family might plant a memorial garden with flowers that evoke the scent of their loved one's favorite perfume. A museum might create an olfactory exhibit that recreates the smellscape of a particular historical event or period. An artist might create an olfactory installation that explores the themes of loss, grief, and memory.

The use of smell in commemoration can provide a visceral and emotional connection to the deceased, allowing us to experience their presence in a way that transcends the physical realm. It can also create opportunities for shared remembrance and community healing.

The Future of Smell and Death: Ethical Considerations in a Changing World:

The relationship between smell and death is a complex and evolving one. As our understanding of the human olfactory system deepens, and as new technologies emerge for manipulating and recreating smells, we must grapple with the ethical implications of these advancements.

The use of olfactory technologies in mortuary practices, grief counseling, and commemoration raises questions about authenticity, privacy, and the potential for manipulation. It is essential to develop ethical guidelines for the use of these technologies, ensuring that they are used in a way that respects the dignity of the deceased and the needs of mourners.

The changing cultural landscape surrounding death also presents new challenges and opportunities for olfactory engagement. The growing acceptance of natural burial practices, the rise of the death positive movement, and the increasing interest in olfactory heritage are creating new possibilities for using smell to honor the dead, preserve memories, and confront the reality of mortality.

By embracing the power of smell to evoke emotions, trigger memories, and connect us to the past, we can create a more meaningful and compassionate approach to death and dying.

Chapter Fourteen: Animal Ethics and the Olfactory: Interspecies Communication, Factory Farming, and the Right to a Scent-Free Life

The olfactory world of animals is vastly different from our own. Many creatures possess a sense of smell far more acute and nuanced than ours, relying on olfactory cues for a wide range of essential functions, from navigation and foraging to communication and mate selection. This chapter explores the ethical dimensions of our relationship with animals through the lens of smell, examining how our olfactory perceptions shape our interactions with other species, the impact of human activities on the olfactory environments of animals, and the ethical considerations that arise when considering the olfactory well-being of animals in a human-dominated world.

The Language of Scent: Olfactory Communication in the Animal Kingdom:

Smell is a primary mode of communication for many animal species. Animals release a variety of chemical signals, known as pheromones, that convey information about their identity, social status, reproductive status, and even their emotional state. These pheromones can be detected by other members of the same species, triggering specific behavioral or physiological responses.

For example, female moths release pheromones that can attract male moths from miles away, ensuring successful mating. Dogs use urine marking to communicate territorial boundaries and social status. Ants leave pheromone trails to guide other ants to food sources.

The complexity and sophistication of olfactory communication in the animal kingdom are often underestimated by humans, who rely more heavily on visual and auditory cues for communication.

However, a deeper understanding of animal olfaction can provide valuable insights into the social lives, behaviors, and ecological roles of other species.

The Olfactory Worlds of Animals: Experiencing the Smellscape Through Different Noses:

The olfactory experiences of animals can be vastly different from our own, as their olfactory systems are often adapted to detect and interpret specific scents that are relevant to their survival and well-being. Dogs, for example, possess a sense of smell that is estimated to be 10,000 to 100,000 times more sensitive than ours. They have a larger olfactory epithelium, the tissue in the nasal cavity that contains olfactory receptor neurons, and a greater number of olfactory receptors, the proteins that bind to odorant molecules.

This heightened sense of smell allows dogs to detect a wide range of scents that are imperceptible to humans, such as the subtle changes in body odor that can indicate the presence of disease or the faint traces of explosives or narcotics.

Other animals have olfactory systems that are specialized for detecting specific scents that are relevant to their ecological niche. For example, sharks have a highly developed sense of smell that allows them to detect blood in the water from miles away. Bees have olfactory receptors that are tuned to the scents of flowers, guiding them to nectar and pollen sources.

Understanding the olfactory worlds of animals can help us to appreciate the diversity of sensory experiences in the animal kingdom and to recognize the importance of preserving the olfactory environments that are essential for the well-being of other species.

The Impact of Human Activities on Animal Olfaction:

Human activities can have a significant impact on the olfactory environments of animals, disrupting their ability to communicate, navigate, and find food. Air pollution, for example, can mask or distort natural scents, making it difficult for animals to detect pheromones or other olfactory cues.

Noise pollution can also interfere with animal olfaction. Studies have shown that exposure to loud noises can reduce the sensitivity of olfactory receptors, making it harder for animals to detect and interpret smells.

Habitat loss and fragmentation can also disrupt animal olfaction. When natural habitats are destroyed or fragmented, animals may be forced to live in closer proximity to humans, exposing them to a wider range of anthropogenic odors that can interfere with their olfactory communication and navigation.

The use of pesticides and other chemicals in agriculture can also have a negative impact on animal olfaction. These chemicals can directly damage olfactory receptor neurons or mask natural scents, making it difficult for animals to find food or mates.

The Olfactory Suffering of Factory Farm Animals:

Factory farming, the intensive confinement of animals for food production, raises serious ethical concerns about the well-being of animals. The olfactory environment of factory farms is often characterized by a high concentration of ammonia, hydrogen sulfide, and other noxious gases released from animal waste.

These smells can cause respiratory problems, eye irritation, and stress in animals. They can also mask natural scents, making it difficult for animals to communicate with each other or to engage in natural behaviors.

The high density of animals in factory farms also creates a stressful and chaotic olfactory environment. Animals are constantly exposed to the smells of their own waste and the smells of other animals, leading to olfactory overload and sensory deprivation.

The ethical implications of factory farming extend beyond the physical suffering of animals. The denial of animals' basic needs, including the need for a clean and stimulating olfactory environment, raises questions about our moral obligations to other species.

Olfactory Enrichment for Captive Animals:

The recognition of the importance of olfactory stimulation for animal well-being has led to the development of olfactory enrichment programs for captive animals in zoos, aquariums, and other facilities. These programs aim to provide animals with a more diverse and stimulating olfactory environment, mimicking the smellscapes they would encounter in their natural habitats.

Olfactory enrichment can involve introducing a variety of natural scents into the animals' enclosures, such as herbs, spices, flowers, or even the scents of other animals. It can also involve creating opportunities for animals to engage in natural olfactory behaviors, such as scent marking or foraging for hidden food items.

Studies have shown that olfactory enrichment can have a positive impact on the well-being of captive animals, reducing stress, promoting natural behaviors, and even improving their overall health.

The Right to a Scent-Free Life: Ethical Considerations for Companion Animals:

The olfactory experiences of companion animals, such as dogs and cats, are often overlooked by their human caregivers. While we may enjoy the smell of our pets, we may not be aware of the potential for our own olfactory choices to affect their well-being.

The use of strong perfumes, air fresheners, and other scented products in our homes can create an overwhelming and unpleasant olfactory environment for our pets. Their heightened sense of smell makes them more sensitive to these scents, which can cause respiratory problems, allergies, and even behavioral changes.

The ethics of pet ownership require a consideration of the olfactory needs of our companion animals. We should be mindful of the potential impact of our own olfactory choices on their well-being and strive to create a home environment that is both safe and stimulating for their olfactory senses.

The Smell of Fear: Olfactory Stress and Animal Welfare:

The smell of fear, a phenomenon well-documented in the animal kingdom, highlights the powerful impact of olfactory cues on animal emotions and behavior. When animals are stressed or frightened, they release pheromones that can be detected by other members of their species, triggering a fear response and potentially leading to a cascade of panic or aggression.

The smell of fear can be particularly problematic in situations where animals are confined in close quarters, such as in shelters, laboratories, or transport vehicles. The release of fear pheromones by one animal can quickly spread throughout the group, creating a stressful and potentially dangerous environment.

The ethical implications of the smell of fear extend beyond the immediate well-being of animals. The chronic exposure to stress and fear can have long-term negative impacts on animal health, behavior, and reproductive success.

Animal welfare guidelines should take into account the olfactory dimensions of stress and fear, promoting management practices that minimize the potential for olfactory stress in captive animals.

Olfactory Ethics and the Future of Human-Animal Relations:

The olfactory dimension of our relationship with animals is often overlooked in ethical discussions about animal welfare and animal rights. However, a deeper understanding of animal olfaction can provide valuable insights into the needs, experiences, and vulnerabilities of other species.

Olfactory ethics, an emerging field of inquiry, seeks to address the ethical questions that arise from our olfactory interactions with animals. This includes considering the impact of human activities on the olfactory environments of animals, the olfactory suffering of animals in factory farms and other confined settings, and the ethical obligations we have to provide animals with a clean, stimulating, and safe olfactory environment.

The future of human-animal relations requires a more nuanced and compassionate understanding of the olfactory world of animals. By recognizing the importance of smell in the lives of other species, we can promote more ethical and sustainable practices in animal agriculture, wildlife management, and companion animal care.

The development of olfactory enrichment programs for captive animals, the reduction of air pollution and noise pollution, and the promotion of sustainable farming practices can all contribute to a more olfactory-friendly world for animals.

By embracing the principles of olfactory ethics, we can move towards a more harmonious and respectful relationship with the animal kingdom, recognizing the intrinsic value of all creatures and their right to a life free from olfactory suffering.

Chapter Fifteen: The Ethics of Olfactory Art: Aesthetics, Perception, and the Moral Responsibilities of the Smell Artist

Art, in its myriad forms, has long sought to engage our senses, evoke emotions, and challenge our perceptions of the world. While visual art, music, and literature have traditionally dominated the artistic landscape, the sense of smell, often relegated to the periphery of aesthetic experience, has recently emerged as a powerful and evocative medium for artistic exploration. This chapter delves into the burgeoning field of olfactory art, examining the unique challenges and opportunities presented by smell as an artistic medium, the ethical considerations that arise when creating and experiencing olfactory art, and the potential for smell to expand the boundaries of artistic expression and deepen our engagement with the world around us.

The Ephemeral Art of Scent: Capturing the Elusive Nature of Smell:

Smell, unlike its visual and auditory counterparts, is inherently ephemeral and elusive. Scents dissipate quickly, their intensity and character changing over time, making it challenging to capture and preserve olfactory experiences in a traditional artistic format. This ephemeral nature of smell has historically limited its use as an artistic medium, with visual and auditory art forms often dominating the artistic landscape.

However, the ephemeral nature of smell can also be seen as a source of its artistic power. The fleeting and transient nature of scents can evoke a sense of immediacy, intimacy, and even vulnerability, creating a unique and visceral connection between the artwork and the audience.

Smell artists have developed a variety of techniques for capturing and manipulating scents, from the use of essential oils and natural materials to the creation of synthetic odorants and the deployment of scent diffusion technologies. These techniques allow artists to create olfactory compositions that evoke specific emotions, memories, or even abstract concepts.

The Subjectivity of Smell: Navigating the Perceptual Landscape of Olfactory Art:

The perception of smell is highly subjective, influenced by individual differences in olfactory sensitivity, cultural backgrounds, and personal experiences. What one person finds pleasant and evocative, another may find repulsive or even offensive. This subjectivity of smell presents unique challenges for olfactory artists, who must navigate a diverse and unpredictable perceptual landscape.

Smell artists often embrace the subjectivity of smell as a source of creative inspiration. They may intentionally create olfactory works that evoke a range of responses, inviting the audience to engage with the artwork on a personal and emotional level. They may also explore the cultural and social meanings associated with different smells, using scent to challenge or subvert traditional olfactory norms.

The subjectivity of smell also raises questions about the role of the audience in olfactory art. Unlike visual or auditory art, which can be passively observed or listened to, olfactory art requires active participation from the audience. The audience must engage their olfactory senses, actively sniffing and interpreting the scents presented to them. This active participation can create a more immersive and interactive artistic experience.

Olfactory Aesthetics: Defining the Beauty and Meaning of Smell in Art:

The aesthetics of smell, the principles that govern the beauty and meaning of olfactory experiences in art, are still being developed and debated. Unlike visual art, which has a long and established tradition of aesthetic theory, olfactory art is a relatively new field, and its aesthetic principles are still being explored and defined.

Some olfactory artists draw inspiration from the principles of perfumery, using fragrance notes and olfactory pyramids to create complex and layered olfactory compositions. Others may explore the use of scent to evoke specific emotions, memories, or even abstract concepts.

The aesthetics of smell can also be informed by the principles of environmental psychology, which explores the relationship between humans and their environment, including the olfactory environment. Smell artists may use scent to create immersive and evocative smellscapes that transport the audience to different places or times.

The development of a robust olfactory aesthetic theory is crucial for the advancement of olfactory art as a recognized and respected art form. This theory should take into account the unique properties of smell, its subjective nature, and its potential to evoke a wide range of emotional and cognitive responses.

The Ethics of Olfactory Art: Responsibility, Consent, and the Potential for Harm:

The creation and experience of olfactory art raise ethical considerations that are unique to this emerging art form. Smell artists have a responsibility to consider the potential impact of their work on the audience, both physically and psychologically.

Some scents can trigger allergic reactions or sensitivities in certain individuals. Smell artists should be mindful of these potential risks and take steps to minimize the likelihood of harm, such as providing clear warnings about the use of potentially allergenic ingredients or offering alternative scent-free experiences.

The use of scent to evoke strong emotions or memories also raises ethical concerns. Smell artists should be cautious about using scent to manipulate or exploit the emotions of the audience, particularly in situations where individuals may be vulnerable or susceptible to suggestion.

The ethics of olfactory art also involve considerations of consent. The audience should be informed about the nature of the olfactory experience they are about to engage in and given the opportunity to opt out if they are uncomfortable or have concerns about potential health risks.

Olfactory Art and Social Justice: Smell as a Tool for Social Commentary and Change:

Olfactory art can be a powerful tool for social commentary and change. Smell artists can use scent to raise awareness of social issues, challenge dominant narratives, and promote empathy and understanding.

For example, smell artists have used scent to explore themes of environmental pollution, poverty, and social inequality. They have also used scent to create olfactory memorials to victims of violence and injustice.

The use of smell in social commentary can be particularly effective in engaging the audience on an emotional and visceral level. Smell can bypass the cognitive filters that we often use to process information, creating a more immediate and powerful connection to the issue at hand.

Olfactory art can also be used to promote social change by creating olfactory experiences that challenge our assumptions and prejudices. For example, smell artists have used scent to explore themes of race, gender, and sexuality, challenging traditional olfactory stereotypes and promoting greater understanding and acceptance of diversity.

Olfactory Art and the Museum: Integrating Smell into the Cultural Landscape:

The integration of olfactory art into museums and other cultural institutions presents both challenges and opportunities. Museums have traditionally been focused on visual and auditory art forms, and the incorporation of smell into museum exhibits requires a rethinking of traditional museum practices and display strategies.

One of the main challenges is the technical difficulty of presenting olfactory art in a museum setting. Smell is a fleeting and ephemeral phenomenon, and the control and containment of scents in a museum environment can be challenging.

Museums have experimented with a variety of methods for presenting olfactory art, from the use of scent diffusers and olfactory displays to the creation of olfactory installations and immersive smellscapes. The choice of method often depends on the specific artwork being presented and the desired audience experience.

The integration of olfactory art into museums can enhance the visitor experience, providing a more multisensory and engaging encounter with art and culture. It can also expand the boundaries of artistic expression, challenging traditional notions of what constitutes art and opening up new possibilities for creativity and innovation.

The Future of Olfactory Art: Expanding the Boundaries of Artistic Expression:

Olfactory art is a rapidly evolving field, with new technologies and artistic approaches emerging that are pushing the boundaries of olfactory expression. Advances in synthetic biology, for example, are creating new possibilities for designing and engineering bespoke scents, allowing artists to create olfactory experiences that are tailored to specific themes, emotions, or even individual audience members.

Virtual reality and augmented reality technologies are also being explored as platforms for olfactory art, creating immersive and interactive smellscapes that can transport the audience to different places or times.

The development of olfactory technologies, such as electronic noses and olfactory sensors, is also providing new tools for artists to capture, analyze, and manipulate scents, opening up new possibilities for olfactory composition and performance.

The future of olfactory art is full of potential. As the field continues to evolve, we can expect to see even more innovative and thought-provoking olfactory artworks that challenge our perceptions, expand our understanding of the world, and deepen our appreciation for the power of smell.

The exploration of smell as an artistic medium is still in its early stages, but it holds immense promise for enriching the artistic landscape and deepening our engagement with the world around us. As we become more attuned to the nuances of our olfactory senses, we can expect to see even more creative and groundbreaking olfactory artworks that challenge our perceptions, evoke powerful emotions, and expand the boundaries of artistic expression.

Chapter Sixteen: Designing Smellscapes: Urban Planning, Architecture, and the Ethics of Olfactory Environments

The cities we inhabit are not just visual and auditory landscapes; they are also complex olfactory environments, shaped by a multitude of scents emanating from human activities, natural elements, and the built environment itself. This chapter explores the emerging field of olfactory urbanism, examining how smell is becoming an increasingly important consideration in urban planning and architectural design. We will delve into the ethical dimensions of designing smellscapes, the conscious and deliberate shaping of olfactory environments in urban spaces, and the potential for smell to enhance the quality of life, promote social equity, and foster a deeper connection between people and their surroundings.

The Olfactory City: Smellscapes as Urban Infrastructure:

The smellscapes of cities are often overlooked in urban planning and design, which have traditionally focused on visual aesthetics and functional considerations. However, smell plays a crucial role in shaping our perceptions of urban spaces, influencing our emotions, behaviors, and even our sense of place and belonging.

The smells of a city can be both alluring and repulsive, reflecting the diversity of human activities, the presence of nature, and the impact of industrial processes. The aroma of freshly brewed coffee wafting from a sidewalk cafe, the scent of flowers blooming in a park, or the smell of rain on pavement can evoke positive emotions and create a sense of vibrancy and vitality. Conversely, the stench of exhaust fumes, garbage, or industrial emissions can trigger disgust, anxiety, and even a desire to avoid certain areas.

Olfactory urbanism recognizes the importance of smell as a critical element of urban infrastructure, akin to transportation systems, water networks, and energy grids. Just as these physical infrastructures shape the flow of people, resources, and information within a city, the olfactory landscape shapes our sensory experiences, influences our movements, and contributes to the overall quality of urban life.

Designing Smellscapes: The Conscious Shaping of Olfactory Environments:

Designing smellscapes involves the conscious and deliberate shaping of olfactory environments in urban spaces. This can involve a variety of strategies, including:

- **Source control:** Identifying and mitigating sources of unpleasant smells, such as industrial emissions, traffic exhaust, or garbage disposal facilities.

- **Olfactory zoning:** Designating specific areas for activities that produce strong smells, such as restaurants or food markets, to minimize their impact on surrounding neighborhoods.

- **Olfactory buffers:** Creating green spaces or other physical barriers to separate areas with conflicting smells, such as industrial zones and residential areas.

- **Olfactory enhancement:** Introducing pleasant smells into urban spaces, such as planting fragrant flowers, installing scent diffusers, or incorporating natural materials with pleasant odors into building designs.

- **Olfactory art:** Commissioning olfactory artworks or installations that engage the sense of smell and enhance the aesthetic experience of urban spaces.

Designing smellscapes requires a multidisciplinary approach, involving collaboration between urban planners, architects, landscape designers, environmental engineers, and even smell artists. It also requires a deep understanding of the olfactory perceptions and preferences of the local community, as well as the cultural and historical significance of smell in the specific urban context.

The Ethics of Smellscape Design: Balancing Competing Interests and Values:

The design of smellscapes raises ethical questions about the balance between individual preferences, community values, and the common good. While certain smells may be universally considered pleasant or unpleasant, olfactory perceptions are often subjective and culturally contingent. What one person finds appealing, another may find offensive or even harmful.

For example, the smell of incense might be considered a source of spiritual comfort and tranquility in some cultures, while it might trigger allergic reactions or sensitivities in others. The smell of freshly cut grass might evoke pleasant memories of childhood for some, while it might be associated with allergies and hay fever for others.

The ethics of smellscape design require a careful consideration of these diverse perspectives and a commitment to creating olfactory environments that are inclusive, equitable, and respectful of individual differences. This may involve incorporating a variety of scents into urban spaces, providing options for individuals to avoid exposure to certain smells, and engaging in open dialogue with the community about olfactory preferences and concerns.

Olfactory Justice in Urban Planning: Addressing Environmental Racism and Olfactory Inequality:

The concept of olfactory justice, introduced in Chapter Three, highlights the unequal distribution of olfactory burdens and benefits in urban environments. Historically, marginalized communities, particularly communities of color and low-income communities, have been disproportionately exposed to noxious smells from industrial facilities, waste management sites, and other sources of pollution.

Olfactory justice in urban planning requires addressing this legacy of environmental racism and olfactory inequality. This can involve prioritizing the mitigation of unpleasant smells in marginalized communities, ensuring that these communities have access to green spaces and other olfactory amenities, and engaging in meaningful dialogue with these communities about their olfactory concerns and preferences.

Olfactory justice also requires challenging the dominant olfactory norms that often privilege certain smells while stigmatizing others. For example, the smell of industrial emissions might be tolerated or even ignored in affluent neighborhoods, while the same smell might be considered a major nuisance in a low-income community. Challenging these olfactory hierarchies and promoting a more equitable distribution of olfactory resources is essential for achieving olfactory justice in urban planning.

The Olfactory Dimension of Public Health: Designing Smellscapes for Well-being:

The smellscapes of cities can have a significant impact on public health and well-being. Exposure to noxious smells can cause a range of adverse health effects, including respiratory problems, headaches, nausea, and stress. Conversely, pleasant smells can have a positive impact on mood, cognitive function, and even physical health.

For example, studies have shown that the smell of lavender can have a calming effect, reducing anxiety and promoting relaxation. The smell of citrus can be energizing and uplifting, improving mood and cognitive performance. The smell of nature, such as the scent of trees or flowers, has been shown to reduce stress and improve overall well-being.

Designing smellscapes with public health in mind involves considering the potential impact of different smells on human physiology and psychology. This can involve incorporating scents that have been shown to have positive health benefits, such as lavender or citrus, into public spaces. It can also involve mitigating sources of unpleasant smells that can have negative health impacts, such as industrial emissions or traffic exhaust.

Olfactory Wayfinding: Using Smell to Navigate Urban Spaces:

Smell can play a role in wayfinding, the process of navigating and orienting oneself in an environment. Our olfactory sense can provide cues that help us to identify specific locations, distinguish between different areas, and even create a sense of familiarity and belonging in a particular place.

For example, the smell of freshly baked bread might help us to locate a bakery, the scent of chlorine might indicate the presence of a swimming pool, or the smell of pine needles might guide us to a park or forest.

Urban planners and architects can use smell to enhance wayfinding in urban spaces. This can involve incorporating scents that are associated with specific locations or activities into the design of buildings, public spaces, or even transportation systems. For example, a hospital might use a calming scent like lavender in waiting areas to reduce anxiety and promote a sense of tranquility. A shopping mall might use a stimulating scent like citrus in common areas to encourage shoppers to linger and explore.

Olfactory wayfinding can be particularly beneficial for individuals with visual impairments, who may rely more heavily on their other senses, including smell, to navigate their surroundings. Designing urban spaces with olfactory cues in mind can enhance accessibility and inclusivity for all members of the community.

The Olfactory Dimension of Placemaking: Creating a Sense of Identity and Belonging Through Smell:

Placemaking, the process of creating public spaces that are meaningful and engaging for the local community, often focuses on visual aesthetics and social interactions. However, smell can also play a crucial role in creating a sense of place and fostering a deeper connection between people and their surroundings.

The smellscapes of a place can contribute to its unique identity and character. For example, the smell of salt air and seafood might be associated with a coastal town, the aroma of coffee and spices might characterize a bustling urban neighborhood, or the scent of pine needles and fresh air might define a mountain resort.

Urban planners and architects can use smell to enhance placemaking in urban spaces. This can involve incorporating scents that are associated with the local history, culture, or environment into the design of public spaces, buildings, or even events. For example, a city might plant trees or flowers that are native to the region to create a smellscape that reflects the local ecosystem. A historical district might recreate the smells of a bygone era, such as the scent of horses and carriages or the aroma of coal-fired stoves, to evoke a sense of the past.

Olfactory placemaking can also involve engaging the local community in the design and implementation of smellscape interventions. This can include conducting surveys or focus groups to gather feedback on olfactory preferences, organizing community workshops to explore the cultural significance of smell in the local context, or even commissioning olfactory artworks or installations that reflect the unique identity of the place.

Olfactory Architecture: Integrating Smell into the Design of Buildings and Spaces:

Olfactory architecture, an emerging field within architectural design, explores the integration of smell into the design of buildings and interior spaces. Architects are beginning to recognize the potential for smell to enhance the aesthetic experience of buildings, influence mood and behavior, and even contribute to the overall functionality of spaces.

The use of natural materials with pleasant odors, such as wood, stone, or even certain types of paint, can create a more welcoming and inviting atmosphere in a building. The strategic placement of scent diffusers or the incorporation of olfactory elements into ventilation systems can also be used to create specific olfactory zones within a building, such as a calming scent in a waiting area or a stimulating scent in a workspace.

Olfactory architecture can also be used to create a sense of continuity between the interior and exterior of a building. For example, a building might incorporate the scent of the surrounding landscape, such as the smell of the ocean or a nearby forest, into its interior design to create a seamless transition between the indoors and outdoors.

The design of olfactory architecture requires a deep understanding of the human olfactory system, the psychology of smell, and the principles of architectural design. It also requires a sensitivity to the cultural and social meanings associated with different smells and the potential impact of olfactory interventions on the users of the space.

The Future of Olfactory Urbanism: Towards a More Fragrant and Equitable City:

The field of olfactory urbanism is still in its early stages of development, but it holds immense potential for transforming the way we design and experience cities. As our understanding of the human olfactory system deepens, and as new technologies emerge for capturing, manipulating, and diffusing scents, we can expect to see even more innovative and creative approaches to smellscape design.

The future of olfactory urbanism will likely involve a greater emphasis on sustainability, inclusivity, and community engagement. Designers will need to consider the environmental impacts of olfactory interventions, ensuring that the use of scents does not contribute to air pollution or other environmental problems. They will also need to be mindful of the diverse olfactory preferences of the community, creating smellscapes that are welcoming and accessible to all.

The development of olfactory technologies, such as electronic noses and olfactory sensors, may also play a role in the future of olfactory urbanism. These technologies could be used to monitor and analyze the smellscapes of cities, providing valuable data that can inform urban planning and design decisions.

The integration of smell into virtual and augmented reality environments may also create new possibilities for experiencing and designing urban spaces. Imagine being able to take a virtual tour of a city and experience its unique smellscape, or using augmented reality to overlay olfactory information onto your real-world view of a city.

The future of olfactory urbanism is full of exciting possibilities. By embracing the power of smell to enhance the quality of life, promote social equity, and foster a deeper connection between people and their surroundings, we can create cities that are not just visually appealing but also olfactory rich and engaging for all.

Chapter Seventeen: The Future of Smell: Technology, Olfactory Enhancement, and the Ethical Challenges of a Synthetic Olfactory World

The human relationship with smell is poised for a dramatic transformation in the coming years, driven by rapid advancements in technology and a growing understanding of the intricate workings of the olfactory system. From devices that can digitally capture and recreate scents to implantable technologies that could enhance or even restore the sense of smell, the future of olfaction is pregnant with possibilities – and ethical dilemmas. This chapter explores the emerging technologies that are reshaping our olfactory world, examining the potential benefits and risks of these innovations, and the ethical challenges we face as we navigate a future where smell can be manipulated, augmented, and even synthetically generated.

The Digitalization of Smell: Capturing and Recreating Olfactory Experiences:

One of the most significant advancements in olfactory technology is the ability to digitally capture and recreate scents. This involves using sensors to analyze the volatile organic compounds (VOCs) that create a particular smell, creating a digital "fingerprint" of the odor. This fingerprint can then be used to recreate the smell using a device called an olfactory display, which releases a combination of odorants that mimic the original scent.

Several companies are developing olfactory displays for a variety of applications, including:

- **Entertainment:** Imagine watching a movie and being able to smell the freshly baked bread in a bakery scene, the salty air of the ocean in a beach scene, or even the fear-inducing scent of a monster's breath in a horror movie. Olfactory displays could add a new dimension of immersion and realism to movies, video games, and other forms of entertainment.

- **Virtual Reality (VR) and Augmented Reality (AR):** Olfactory displays could be integrated into VR and AR headsets, allowing users to experience the smells of virtual environments or to enhance their perception of the real world with digitally generated scents. This could revolutionize the way we interact with virtual worlds and could have applications in fields such as education, training, and therapy.

- **Communication:** Imagine being able to send a "smell message" to a friend or loved one, allowing them to experience the scent of a freshly picked flower, a favorite perfume, or even a home-cooked meal. Olfactory displays could add a new dimension to digital communication, allowing us to share olfactory experiences across distances.

- **Marketing and Retail:** Olfactory displays are already being used in some retail environments to create a more immersive and engaging shopping experience. Imagine walking into a clothing store and being able to smell the fresh scent of cotton, the leather of a new jacket, or the perfume that a model is wearing in an advertisement. Olfactory displays could be used to create a more enticing and memorable shopping experience, potentially influencing consumer behavior.

Olfactory Enhancement: Augmenting and Restoring the Sense of Smell:

Another promising area of olfactory technology is the development of devices and therapies that can enhance or even restore the sense of smell. These technologies could have a profound impact on the lives of individuals with olfactory impairments, such as anosmia (the loss of the sense of smell) or hyposmia (a reduced sense of smell).

Some of the technologies being developed for olfactory enhancement include:

- **Electronic Noses:** Electronic noses are devices that use sensors to detect and analyze smells. They are being developed for a variety of applications, including medical diagnosis, environmental monitoring, and food safety. Electronic noses could also be used to create personalized olfactory profiles, allowing individuals to track their own sense of smell over time and to identify potential olfactory impairments.

- **Olfactory Implants:** Olfactory implants are devices that are surgically implanted into the nasal cavity and stimulate the olfactory nerve, sending signals to the brain that are interpreted as smell. These implants are still in the early stages of development, but they hold the potential to restore the sense of smell in individuals with anosmia or hyposmia.

- **Gene Therapy:** Gene therapy involves introducing new genes into cells to treat or prevent diseases. Researchers are exploring the possibility of using gene therapy to restore the function of olfactory receptor neurons in individuals with olfactory impairments.

- **Olfactory Training:** Olfactory training involves repeated exposure to different scents to improve olfactory sensitivity and discrimination. This therapy has been shown to be effective in improving the sense of smell in some individuals with olfactory impairments.

The Ethical Challenges of a Synthetic Olfactory World:

The ability to digitally capture, recreate, and even enhance the sense of smell raises a host of ethical questions that we must grapple with as we move towards a future where smell can be increasingly manipulated and controlled.

Some of the ethical challenges we face include:

- **Authenticity and Deception:** The ability to digitally recreate scents raises questions about the authenticity of olfactory experiences. If we can perfectly recreate the smell of a freshly baked apple pie, does that mean we are experiencing the "real" smell of the pie, or is it merely a simulation? Could olfactory displays be used to deceive people into believing they are smelling something that is not actually present, such as the smell of a clean room in a hotel that is actually quite dirty?

- **Privacy and Surveillance:** The development of electronic noses and other olfactory sensors raises concerns about the potential for olfactory surveillance. Could these technologies be used to track individuals' movements, monitor their health, or even detect their emotions? Could olfactory data be collected and used without individuals' knowledge or consent?

- **Manipulation and Control:** The ability to manipulate and control smells raises concerns about the potential for these technologies to be used for manipulative purposes. Could olfactory displays be used to influence consumer behavior, create a sense of fear or anxiety, or even trigger specific memories or emotions?

- **Accessibility and Equity:** The development of olfactory enhancement technologies raises questions about accessibility and equity. Will these technologies be available to everyone, or will they be primarily accessible to those who can afford them? Could olfactory enhancement technologies exacerbate existing social inequalities?

- **The Natural vs. the Synthetic:** The increasing ability to manipulate and control smells raises questions about the value of natural olfactory experiences. If we can create any smell we want, will we lose our appreciation for the natural smellscapes of the world around us? Could the overuse of synthetic scents lead to a form of olfactory sensory overload?

Navigating the Olfactory Future: Ethical Considerations for a Synthetic Smellscape:

As we move towards a future where smell can be increasingly manipulated and controlled, it is crucial to develop ethical guidelines and regulations that ensure these technologies are used responsibly and ethically.

Some of the key ethical considerations include:

- **Transparency and Informed Consent:** Individuals should be informed about the use of olfactory technologies and given the opportunity to opt out of exposure to synthetic scents or olfactory surveillance. Companies that develop and deploy olfactory technologies should be transparent about the capabilities and limitations of these technologies and the potential risks associated with their use.

- **Data Security and Privacy:** Olfactory data should be treated with the same level of care and protection as other forms of personal data. Companies that collect and store olfactory data should implement robust security measures to prevent unauthorized access or misuse of this data.

- **Responsible Innovation:** Companies that develop olfactory technologies should prioritize responsible innovation, considering the potential ethical and societal implications of their products and services. They should engage in open dialogue with ethicists, policymakers, and the public to ensure that these technologies are developed and deployed in a way that benefits society as a whole.

- **Olfactory Literacy and Education:** Promoting olfactory literacy, the ability to identify, understand, and appreciate a diverse range of smells, is essential for navigating a future where smell can be increasingly manipulated and controlled. Educating people about the science of olfaction, the cultural significance of smell, and the ethical implications of olfactory technologies can empower them to make informed decisions about their own olfactory experiences and to participate in the broader societal conversation about the future of smell.

The Future of Smell: Embracing the Opportunities, Addressing the Challenges:

The future of smell is full of both exciting opportunities and complex challenges. The ability to digitally capture and recreate scents, to enhance or restore the sense of smell, and to design and manipulate olfactory environments has the potential to revolutionize a wide range of fields, from entertainment and communication to healthcare and urban planning.

However, it is crucial that we approach these technological advancements with a thoughtful and ethical lens. By carefully considering the potential benefits and risks of olfactory technologies, by developing ethical guidelines and regulations, and by promoting olfactory literacy and education, we can ensure that the future of smell is one that enhances human well-being, promotes social justice, and fosters a deeper appreciation for the rich and complex world of olfaction.

Chapter Eighteen: Olfactory Privacy: The Right to Smell, the Right Not to Smell, and the Ethics of Olfactory Data

The rise of olfactory technology, with its ability to capture, analyze, and manipulate smells, presents new challenges to our understanding and protection of privacy. While traditional notions of privacy have focused on visual and auditory information, the increasing ability to collect and analyze olfactory data raises unique ethical concerns about the right to control our own smells, the right to be free from unwanted olfactory intrusions, and the potential for olfactory data to be used for discriminatory or exploitative purposes. This chapter explores the emerging concept of olfactory privacy, examining the ways in which our sense of smell intersects with our right to privacy, the challenges of protecting olfactory data in a world of ubiquitous sensing, and the implications of olfactory technology for our understanding of personal autonomy and social justice.

The Right to Smell: Olfactory Freedom and the Pursuit of Olfactory Pleasure:

The right to smell encompasses the freedom to experience and enjoy the smellscapes of our world, both natural and artificial. This includes the right to choose the scents we surround ourselves with, whether it's the aroma of our favorite coffee in the morning, the fragrance of a freshly cut lawn, or the perfume we choose to wear.

Olfactory freedom is essential for our well-being and our ability to express our identities. Smell plays a crucial role in our emotional and cognitive experiences, influencing our mood, memory, and even our social interactions. The ability to choose and control the scents we encounter is an important aspect of personal autonomy and self-determination.

However, the right to smell is not absolute. Our olfactory choices can have an impact on others, particularly in shared spaces. The strong perfume we choose to wear might trigger an allergic reaction in someone nearby, the smell of our cooking might permeate into a neighbor's apartment, or the smoke from our cigarette might bother those around us.

Balancing the right to smell with the rights and sensitivities of others is essential for creating a harmonious and equitable olfactory environment. This requires mutual respect, consideration for the impact of our olfactory choices on others, and a willingness to compromise when necessary.

The Right Not to Smell: Olfactory Intrusions and the Protection from Olfactory Harms:

The right not to smell encompasses the right to be free from unwanted olfactory intrusions and the protection from olfactory harms. This includes the right to breathe clean air, free from noxious smells and pollutants, and the right to control the scents that enter our personal spaces.

Olfactory intrusions can range from the mildly annoying, such as the smell of cigarette smoke wafting from a nearby car, to the severely debilitating, such as the stench of raw sewage or industrial emissions. Exposure to unpleasant or harmful smells can cause a range of adverse effects, including headaches, nausea, respiratory problems, and even psychological distress.

Protecting the right not to smell requires a combination of individual responsibility and collective action. Individuals can take steps to minimize their own olfactory impact on others, such as avoiding the use of strong perfumes in enclosed spaces or properly disposing of garbage to prevent odors. Collective action, through government regulations and community initiatives, is also essential for addressing sources of air pollution and creating a more equitable and healthy olfactory environment for all.

The Ethics of Olfactory Data: Privacy Concerns in a World of Ubiquitous Sensing:

The rise of olfactory technology, with its ability to capture, analyze, and manipulate smells, presents new challenges to our understanding and protection of privacy. Olfactory data, the information about our smells that can be collected and analyzed by electronic noses and other olfactory sensors, can reveal a wealth of personal information, including our health status, diet, emotional state, and even our genetic predispositions.

The collection and use of olfactory data raise a number of ethical concerns:

- **Informed Consent:** Individuals should be informed about the collection and use of their olfactory data and given the opportunity to consent to or opt out of this data collection.

- **Data Security and Confidentiality:** Olfactory data should be stored securely and confidentially, with appropriate safeguards in place to prevent unauthorized access or misuse.

- **Purpose Limitation:** Olfactory data should only be collected and used for specific, legitimate purposes, such as medical diagnosis, environmental monitoring, or public safety. It should not be used for discriminatory or exploitative purposes, such as targeted advertising or insurance risk assessment.

- **Data Minimization:** Only the minimum amount of olfactory data necessary to achieve the specified purpose should be collected and stored.

- **Data Retention:** Olfactory data should only be retained for as long as necessary to achieve the specified purpose. Once the purpose has been fulfilled, the data should be securely deleted or anonymized.

The development of ethical guidelines and regulations for the collection, use, and storage of olfactory data is crucial for protecting olfactory privacy in a world of ubiquitous sensing.

Olfactory Profiling: Discrimination and Bias in the Age of Smell Data:

The ability to collect and analyze olfactory data raises concerns about the potential for olfactory profiling, the use of olfactory information to categorize or discriminate against individuals or groups. Just as facial recognition technology has been shown to exhibit racial and gender biases, olfactory profiling could perpetuate existing social inequalities by associating certain smells with particular groups or characteristics.

For example, imagine a scenario where law enforcement agencies use electronic noses to screen individuals for suspicious odors, such as the smell of drugs or explosives. If these technologies are not calibrated properly or if they are based on flawed assumptions about the olfactory profiles of different groups, they could lead to the disproportionate targeting of certain individuals or communities.

Olfactory profiling could also be used in employment, housing, or insurance contexts, leading to discrimination based on an individual's perceived smell. For example, imagine a scenario where a landlord uses an electronic nose to screen potential tenants, rejecting applicants based on their olfactory profile. Or imagine an insurance company using olfactory data to assess an individual's health risks, charging higher premiums to individuals with certain smells that are associated with higher healthcare costs.

The potential for olfactory profiling underscores the need for careful consideration of the ethical implications of olfactory technology and the development of safeguards to prevent its misuse for discriminatory purposes.

Olfactory Marketing: The Manipulation of Smell and the Erosion of Consumer Autonomy:

Olfactory marketing, the use of smell to influence consumer behavior, is becoming increasingly sophisticated and pervasive. Retailers are using scent diffusers to create specific olfactory atmospheres in their stores, product designers are incorporating scents into their products, and marketers are even using olfactory cues in advertising to trigger specific emotions or memories.

While some olfactory marketing techniques may be relatively benign, such as using the smell of freshly baked bread to create a welcoming atmosphere in a bakery, others raise concerns about the manipulation of consumer behavior and the erosion of consumer autonomy.

For example, imagine a scenario where a casino uses olfactory displays to release scents that are known to increase risk-taking behavior. Or imagine a grocery store using olfactory cues to trigger cravings for unhealthy foods. These olfactory manipulations could exploit our subconscious responses to smells, potentially influencing our choices in ways that we are not even aware of.

The ethics of olfactory marketing require a balance between the interests of businesses and the rights of consumers. Consumers should be informed about the use of olfactory marketing techniques and given the opportunity to opt out of exposure to these manipulations. Regulatory frameworks may also be necessary to prevent the use of olfactory marketing techniques that are deceptive, manipulative, or harmful to consumer well-being.

Olfactory Nuisances and the Right to a Pleasant Smellscape:

The increasing ability to manipulate and control smells raises questions about the right to a pleasant smellscape, free from unwanted olfactory intrusions. While traditional notions of property rights have focused on visual and auditory nuisances, the growing use of olfactory technologies could lead to new forms of olfactory trespass.

For example, imagine a scenario where a neighbor uses an olfactory display to release strong and unpleasant scents into your yard, interfering with your enjoyment of your property. Or imagine a company using olfactory displays to create a pervasive and inescapable olfactory advertisement that follows you throughout your day.

The legal and ethical frameworks for addressing olfactory nuisances are still being developed. Traditional nuisance laws may need to be updated to account for the unique properties of smell and the potential for olfactory technologies to create new forms of olfactory harm.

Olfactory Art and the Boundaries of Privacy:

Olfactory art, the use of smell as an artistic medium, raises questions about the boundaries of privacy in artistic expression. Smell artists often use scents that are personal and evocative, triggering memories, emotions, and even visceral reactions in the audience.

While olfactory art can be a powerful and moving form of artistic expression, it is important to consider the potential impact of these olfactory experiences on the audience. Some scents can be triggering or even traumatic for individuals with certain experiences or sensitivities. Smell artists have a responsibility to be mindful of these potential impacts and to obtain informed consent from the audience before exposing them to potentially sensitive or evocative scents.

The ethics of olfactory art also require a consideration of the context in which the artwork is presented. Olfactory art that might be considered acceptable in a gallery setting might be considered intrusive or even offensive in a public space. Smell artists should be sensitive to the cultural norms and expectations of the community in which their work is presented and should take steps to minimize the potential for olfactory harm or discomfort.

Olfactory Privacy and the Future of Smell:

The concept of olfactory privacy is still evolving as olfactory technology advances and our understanding of the social and ethical implications of smell deepens. The right to control our own smells, the right to be free from unwanted olfactory intrusions, and the right to privacy over our olfactory data are all essential for protecting our personal autonomy and ensuring that olfactory technologies are used ethically and responsibly.

As we navigate the olfactory future, it is crucial to engage in open dialogue about the ethical challenges of a synthetic olfactory world. This dialogue should involve scientists, technologists, policymakers, ethicists, and the public, working together to develop ethical guidelines, regulatory frameworks, and social norms that ensure the responsible and equitable use of olfactory technologies.

The future of smell holds immense potential for enriching our lives, enhancing our understanding of the world, and fostering new forms of human connection. By embracing the principles of olfactory privacy, we can harness the power of smell while safeguarding our individual rights and ensuring that the olfactory landscape of the future is one that is both fragrant and just.

Chapter Nineteen: The Smell of War: Chemical Weapons, Olfactory Trauma, and the Ethics of Olfactory Violence

The pungent smell of cordite after a firefight, the sickeningly sweet stench of mustard gas, the acrid odor of burning flesh – war, in all its brutality, is an intensely olfactory experience. Smell, often overlooked in accounts of armed conflict, plays a powerful and often traumatic role in the lives of soldiers and civilians caught in the throes of war. This chapter explores the unique olfactory dimensions of warfare, examining the use of chemical weapons, the psychological impact of olfactory trauma, and the ethical challenges of deploying olfactory weapons and technologies in the context of armed conflict.

Chemical Warfare: The Weaponization of Smell and the Perversion of Olfaction:

The deliberate use of toxic chemicals to harm or kill has a long and disturbing history, dating back to ancient times. From the use of smoke and burning sulfur to create confusion and panic on the battlefield to the deployment of poisonous gases in siege warfare, smell has long been exploited as a weapon of war.

The 20th century witnessed a dramatic escalation in the development and deployment of chemical weapons, culminating in the horrific use of chlorine, phosgene, and mustard gas during World War I. These chemical agents, designed to inflict excruciating pain and debilitating injuries, left an indelible mark on the olfactory landscape of war, forever associating certain smells with the horrors of industrialized warfare.

Mustard gas, a particularly insidious chemical weapon, caused severe blistering of the skin, eyes, and respiratory tract, leaving victims with agonizing burns and long-term health complications. The smell of mustard gas, often described as a mixture of garlic, horseradish, and mustard, became a symbol of the indiscriminate

121

cruelty of chemical warfare, haunting the memories of soldiers and civilians who experienced its effects.

The use of chemical weapons in World War I sparked international outrage and led to the development of the Geneva Protocol in 1925, which prohibited the use of chemical and biological weapons in warfare. However, despite this international agreement, the development and stockpiling of chemical weapons continued throughout the 20th century, with several countries, including Iraq and Syria, using these weapons against their own citizens or in regional conflicts.

The use of chemical weapons represents a perversion of olfaction, turning our sense of smell, designed to warn us of danger and enhance our experiences of the world, into a source of terror and suffering. The ethical condemnation of chemical warfare is rooted in the recognition that these weapons inflict indiscriminate and disproportionate harm, violating the fundamental principles of humanity and the laws of war.

Olfactory Trauma: The Lingering Scars of War in the Smellscape of Memory:

The smells of war can leave lasting psychological scars on soldiers and civilians, triggering flashbacks, nightmares, and anxiety long after the conflict has ended. Olfactory trauma, a form of post-traumatic stress disorder (PTSD) specific to olfactory experiences, occurs when certain smells become associated with traumatic events, evoking a visceral and often debilitating emotional response.

The smells that trigger olfactory trauma can vary widely, depending on the individual's experiences and the specific context of the trauma. For some veterans, the smell of diesel fuel might evoke memories of riding in a convoy that was ambushed, the scent of burning rubber might trigger flashbacks to a roadside bomb explosion, or the smell of blood might conjure up images of a fallen comrade.

For civilians caught in the crossfire of war, the smells of their destroyed homes, the scent of smoke and debris, or the odor of decaying bodies can become deeply embedded in their olfactory memories, haunting them with reminders of the violence and loss they have experienced.

Olfactory trauma can be a debilitating condition, interfering with daily life, social interactions, and emotional well-being. Individuals with olfactory trauma may avoid certain smells, places, or even people that trigger their traumatic memories. They may also experience a heightened sensitivity to smells, finding even everyday scents overwhelming or distressing.

The treatment of olfactory trauma often involves a combination of therapies, including cognitive behavioral therapy (CBT), exposure therapy, and medication. CBT helps individuals to identify and challenge negative thoughts and beliefs associated with their traumatic memories, while exposure therapy gradually exposes them to the triggering smells in a safe and controlled environment. Medication can help to manage the symptoms of anxiety and depression that often accompany olfactory trauma.

The Smell of Fear: Olfactory Cues and the Psychology of Warfare:

The smell of fear, a phenomenon well-documented in the animal kingdom, also plays a role in human warfare. When individuals are in a state of fear or stress, their bodies release pheromones, chemical signals that can be detected by others, triggering a similar fear response. This olfactory communication of fear can contribute to a cascade of panic or aggression, particularly in the chaotic and unpredictable environment of a battlefield.

The smell of fear can also be used as a tactic of psychological warfare. By intentionally releasing scents that are associated with fear or disgust, such as the smell of decaying bodies or the stench of sewage, combatants can attempt to demoralize or disorient their enemies.

The use of olfactory cues to manipulate emotions and behavior in warfare raises ethical concerns about the exploitation of our primal olfactory instincts. The deliberate infliction of fear or disgust through smell can be considered a form of psychological torture, violating the dignity and well-being of those targeted.

The Ethics of Olfactory Weapons: Non-Lethal Technologies and the Potential for Misuse:

Advances in olfactory technology are creating new possibilities for developing non-lethal weapons that use smell to incapacitate or disorient targets without causing lasting physical harm. These olfactory weapons, often referred to as "malodorants," release highly unpleasant smells that can cause nausea, vomiting, headaches, and disorientation.

While proponents of malodorants argue that they offer a less harmful alternative to traditional lethal weapons, critics raise concerns about the potential for these technologies to be misused for torture or other forms of cruel, inhuman, or degrading treatment.

The use of malodorants also raises questions about the ethical boundaries of sensory manipulation in warfare. While the use of non-lethal weapons is generally considered more acceptable than the use of lethal force, the deliberate infliction of unpleasant sensory experiences, even if they do not cause lasting physical harm, can still be considered a violation of human dignity.

The development and deployment of olfactory weapons require careful ethical consideration, taking into account the potential for misuse, the long-term psychological effects on those exposed, and the broader implications for the conduct of warfare.

Olfactory Surveillance: Sniffing Out Threats and the Erosion of Privacy in War Zones:

Olfactory technology is also being used for surveillance purposes in war zones, with electronic noses and other olfactory sensors being deployed to detect explosives, narcotics, and even human presence. These technologies offer the potential to enhance security and protect soldiers and civilians from harm.

However, the use of olfactory surveillance in war zones also raises privacy concerns. The ability to detect and analyze smells can reveal a wealth of personal information, including an individual's health status, diet, and even their emotional state. The widespread deployment of olfactory sensors in war zones could lead to the collection of vast amounts of personal data, with potential implications for individual privacy and civil liberties.

The use of olfactory surveillance in war zones requires a careful balance between security needs and the protection of individual privacy. Transparency, accountability, and independent oversight are essential to ensure that these technologies are used responsibly and ethically, minimizing the potential for misuse or abuse.

Olfactory Justice in Post-Conflict Recovery: Addressing Olfactory Trauma and Environmental Contamination:

The olfactory legacy of war can linger long after the fighting has ended. Olfactory trauma can continue to affect the lives of veterans and civilians for years or even decades after the conflict. Environmental contamination from chemical weapons, unexploded ordnance, and industrial pollution can also create lingering olfactory hazards, affecting the health and well-being of communities.

Olfactory justice in post-conflict recovery requires addressing these olfactory legacies of war. This includes providing access to mental health services for individuals with olfactory trauma, supporting community-based initiatives to mitigate environmental contamination, and promoting research into the long-term health effects of exposure to wartime olfactory hazards.

Olfactory justice also requires recognizing the cultural and symbolic significance of smell in post-conflict recovery. The smellscapes of war-torn communities can be deeply affected by the violence and destruction they have experienced. The restoration of traditional smellscapes, through the planting of fragrant gardens, the rebuilding of markets and shops, or the reintroduction of traditional culinary practices, can contribute to a sense of healing and renewal.

The Future of Smell and War: Ethical Considerations in a Changing Olfactory Landscape:

The future of warfare will likely be shaped by continued advancements in olfactory technology, offering new possibilities for both enhancing security and inflicting harm. The development of more sophisticated olfactory weapons, the increasing use of olfactory surveillance, and the potential for manipulating smells to influence emotions and behavior on the battlefield all raise profound ethical challenges.

As we navigate this changing olfactory landscape, it is crucial to engage in open dialogue about the ethical implications of these technologies. This dialogue should involve scientists, technologists, military leaders, ethicists, and the public, working together to develop ethical guidelines, international agreements, and regulatory frameworks that ensure the responsible and humane use of olfactory technologies in warfare.

The smells of war have long been associated with suffering, fear, and loss. However, smell can also be a source of healing, resilience, and hope. By recognizing the powerful impact of smell on the human experience of war, we can work towards a future where olfactory technologies are used to mitigate the harms of conflict, promote peace and reconciliation, and create a more just and fragrant world for all.

Chapter Twenty: Olfactory Disabilities: Anosmia, Sensory Deprivation, and the Ethics of Olfactory Inclusion

The world of smell, so rich and multifaceted for many, remains an uncharted territory for those living with olfactory disabilities. Anosmia, the complete loss of the sense of smell, and hyposmia, a reduced sense of smell, can profoundly impact an individual's quality of life, affecting not only their ability to experience the pleasures of food and fragrance but also their safety, social interactions, and emotional well-being. This chapter explores the lived experiences of individuals with olfactory disabilities, the ethical implications of sensory deprivation, and the imperative for creating a more inclusive and accessible world that recognizes and accommodates the needs of those who navigate life without the sense of smell.

Living Without Smell: An Invisible Disability with Profound Impacts

Anosmia and hyposmia, often referred to as "invisible disabilities," can result from a variety of causes, including head injuries, viral infections, nasal polyps, certain medications, and even aging. Despite their prevalence, affecting an estimated 5% of the population, olfactory disabilities often go undiagnosed and misunderstood. Individuals with these conditions may struggle to articulate the impact of their sensory loss, facing skepticism or even disbelief from others who may perceive smell as a less essential sense compared to sight or hearing.

The lack of awareness and understanding of olfactory disabilities can lead to a sense of isolation and frustration for those affected. Individuals with anosmia or hyposmia may feel like they are living in a world that is muted and incomplete, unable to fully participate in the sensory experiences that others take for granted. They may miss out on the joy of savoring a delicious meal, the comfort of a loved one's familiar scent, or the warning signal of smoke or gas leaks.

The impact of olfactory disabilities extends beyond the realm of sensory pleasure. Smell plays a crucial role in our safety and well-being, alerting us to potential dangers such as spoiled food, gas leaks, or fires. Individuals with anosmia or hyposmia may be at increased risk of these hazards, as they lack this crucial olfactory warning system.

Social interactions can also be challenging for individuals with olfactory disabilities. Smell plays a subtle but significant role in our social dynamics, influencing our perceptions of attractiveness, hygiene, and even trustworthiness. Individuals with anosmia or hyposmia may feel self-conscious about their inability to detect body odor or other social cues, leading to anxiety or withdrawal from social situations.

The emotional impact of olfactory disabilities can be profound. Smell is intimately linked to our memories and emotions, and the loss of this sense can lead to feelings of grief, depression, or even a sense of disconnection from the world. Individuals with anosmia or hyposmia may struggle to recall past experiences or to form new memories that are as vivid and emotionally charged as those of individuals with a functional sense of smell.

Sensory Deprivation and the Ethical Imperative of Olfactory Inclusion:

The experiences of individuals with olfactory disabilities highlight the ethical imperative of olfactory inclusion, the recognition and accommodation of the needs of those who navigate life without a functional sense of smell. Sensory deprivation, the lack of access to sensory stimuli, can have a significant impact on cognitive development, emotional well-being, and overall quality of life.

The ethical principle of beneficence, the obligation to do good and prevent harm, calls for us to consider the needs of individuals with olfactory disabilities and to take steps to mitigate the negative impacts of sensory deprivation. This includes promoting awareness and understanding of olfactory disabilities, developing technologies and therapies to enhance or restore the sense of smell, and designing environments that are inclusive and accessible to those who navigate life without a functional sense of smell.

The principle of justice, the fair and equitable treatment of all individuals, also applies to olfactory inclusion. Individuals with olfactory disabilities should have equal opportunities to participate in society, to access education and employment, and to enjoy the same quality of life as those with a functional sense of smell. This requires addressing the social stigma associated with olfactory disabilities, challenging discriminatory practices, and promoting a culture of inclusivity and acceptance.

Designing an Olfactory-Inclusive World: Accommodations and Innovations for Sensory Accessibility:

Creating a more olfactory-inclusive world requires a multi-faceted approach, involving accommodations, innovations, and a shift in societal attitudes towards sensory diversity.

Some of the key areas for action include:

- **Universal Design for Olfaction:** The principles of universal design, which aim to create environments and products that are accessible to people with a wide range of abilities and disabilities, can be applied to the olfactory realm. This includes considering the olfactory needs of individuals with anosmia or hyposmia in the design of buildings, public spaces, and even consumer products.

- **Olfactory Warning Systems:** Developing and implementing olfactory warning systems that use alternative sensory cues, such as visual or auditory signals, to alert individuals with olfactory disabilities to potential dangers such as smoke, gas leaks, or spoiled food.

- **Olfactory Accessibility in Public Spaces:** Creating public spaces that are mindful of the olfactory needs of individuals with anosmia or hyposmia, such as minimizing the use of strong fragrances, providing scent-free zones, and using natural ventilation to improve air quality.

- **Olfactory Education and Training:** Developing educational programs and training materials to raise awareness and understanding of olfactory disabilities, to promote olfactory literacy, and to provide individuals with olfactory disabilities with the skills and strategies they need to navigate a world designed for those with a functional sense of smell.

- **Technological Innovations for Olfactory Enhancement:** Supporting research and development of technologies that can enhance or restore the sense of smell, such as electronic noses, olfactory implants, and gene therapies.

- **Social Inclusion and Anti-Discrimination Measures:** Challenging the social stigma associated with olfactory disabilities, implementing anti-discrimination policies, and promoting a culture of inclusivity and acceptance that recognizes the value and dignity of all individuals, regardless of their sensory abilities.

The Future of Olfactory Inclusion: Embracing Sensory Diversity in a Changing World:

The future of olfactory inclusion will be shaped by ongoing technological advancements, evolving societal attitudes towards disability, and the growing recognition of the importance of sensory diversity. As we move towards a future where smell can be increasingly manipulated and controlled, it is crucial to ensure that these technological advancements are used to benefit all individuals, including those with olfactory disabilities.

The development of olfactory enhancement technologies, such as electronic noses and olfactory implants, has the potential to restore the sense of smell in individuals with anosmia or hyposmia, opening up a world of olfactory experiences that were previously inaccessible to them. However, it is important to ensure that these technologies are accessible and affordable to all who need them, regardless of their socioeconomic status or geographical location.

The design of olfactory-inclusive environments and products will become increasingly important as our understanding of the needs of individuals with olfactory disabilities deepens. This includes considering the olfactory dimensions of universal design, implementing olfactory warning systems, and creating public spaces that are mindful of the diverse olfactory needs of the community.

The promotion of olfactory literacy and education is crucial for creating a more inclusive and understanding society. Educating people about the science of olfaction, the cultural significance of smell, and the lived experiences of individuals with olfactory disabilities can help to break down stereotypes, challenge prejudices, and foster a culture of empathy and acceptance.

The future of olfactory inclusion requires a collective effort from scientists, technologists, policymakers, educators, and the public, working together to create a world that recognizes, accommodates, and celebrates the diversity of human sensory experiences. By embracing the principles of olfactory justice and inclusion, we can create a more fragrant and equitable world for all, regardless of their ability to smell.

Chapter Twenty-One: The Smell of Nature: Environmental Ethics, Wilderness Preservation, and the Right to Experience Natural Scents

The smell of pine needles in a forest, the salty tang of the ocean, the earthy aroma of a freshly plowed field – these natural scents evoke a sense of wonder, tranquility, and connection to the natural world. Our olfactory experiences of nature are deeply intertwined with our emotional and spiritual well-being, shaping our perceptions of the environment, our sense of place, and our understanding of our own place within the web of life. This chapter explores the ethical dimensions of our relationship with the natural smellscape, examining the value of preserving natural scents, the impact of human activities on the olfactory environment, and the right to experience and appreciate the rich diversity of smells that the natural world has to offer.

The Intrinsic Value of Natural Scents: A Biocentric Perspective on Olfactory Heritage:

From a biocentric perspective, which recognizes the intrinsic value of all living beings and ecosystems, natural scents are not merely pleasant or unpleasant sensations; they are essential components of the natural world, playing crucial roles in ecological processes, interspecies communication, and the overall functioning of ecosystems.

The scents released by plants, for example, attract pollinators, deter herbivores, and even communicate with other plants about potential threats or environmental changes. The smells of animals serve a variety of functions, from attracting mates and marking territories to warning of danger and identifying kin. The decomposition of organic matter releases a complex array of scents that contribute to soil fertility and nutrient cycling.

Preserving natural scents, therefore, is not just about protecting human enjoyment of the smellscape; it is about recognizing the intrinsic value of these scents as integral parts of the natural world. Just as we value the visual beauty of a pristine forest or the biodiversity of a coral reef, we should also value the olfactory richness and complexity of these ecosystems.

The Impact of Human Activities on the Natural Smellscape: Pollution, Habitat Loss, and Olfactory Homogenization:

Human activities have profoundly altered the natural smellscape, often with negative consequences for both human and non-human inhabitants of the environment. Air pollution, deforestation, urbanization, and industrial agriculture have all contributed to the degradation and homogenization of natural scents, diminishing the olfactory richness and diversity of the world around us.

Air pollution from vehicles, factories, and power plants releases a cocktail of chemicals into the atmosphere, masking or distorting natural scents and creating an olfactory smog that can be both unpleasant and harmful to human health. The smell of car exhaust, for example, can overpower the delicate scents of wildflowers or the fresh air of a forest, diminishing our ability to fully appreciate the natural smellscape.

Deforestation and habitat loss not only reduce the visual beauty and biodiversity of natural environments but also diminish the olfactory richness of these ecosystems. The clear-cutting of a forest, for example, eliminates the complex blend of scents emanating from trees, undergrowth, and soil, leaving behind a homogenized olfactory landscape dominated by the smell of bare earth or the dust of logging operations.

Urbanization, with its dense concentrations of human activity and built environments, often creates an olfactory environment dominated by anthropogenic scents, such as car exhaust, garbage, and industrial emissions. The natural smellscape is often relegated to small pockets of green space, such as parks or gardens, where the scents of flowers, trees, and soil can provide a brief respite from the olfactory overload of the city.

Industrial agriculture, with its reliance on monocultures, pesticides, and synthetic fertilizers, has also had a significant impact on the natural smellscape. The vast fields of a single crop, such as corn or soybeans, lack the olfactory diversity of a natural prairie or forest. The use of pesticides and herbicides eliminates the scents of wildflowers and other native plants, creating a sterile and homogenized olfactory environment.

The homogenization of the natural smellscape, driven by human activities, not only diminishes our own olfactory experiences of the world but also has implications for the well-being of other species. Animals that rely on olfactory cues for navigation, foraging, mate selection, or communication may be disoriented or confused by the altered smellscape, leading to behavioral changes, reproductive difficulties, or even population decline.

The Right to Experience Natural Scents: An Environmental Justice Perspective on Olfactory Equity:

The right to experience natural scents is an essential aspect of environmental justice, which recognizes the interconnectedness of human well-being and environmental health. Just as we have a right to breathe clean air and drink clean water, we also have a right to experience the full range of sensory experiences that the natural world has to offer, including the rich diversity of natural scents.

This right, however, is not equally distributed. Marginalized communities, particularly communities of color and low-income communities, are often disproportionately exposed to unpleasant or harmful smells from industrial facilities, waste management sites, and other sources of pollution. These communities may also have limited access to green spaces and other natural environments where they can experience the restorative and enriching smells of nature.

Promoting olfactory equity requires addressing these environmental injustices, ensuring that all communities have access to clean air, healthy smellscapes, and opportunities to experience and appreciate the natural world. This can involve prioritizing the mitigation of unpleasant smells in marginalized communities, investing in green spaces and parks, and promoting environmental education programs that foster a deeper understanding and appreciation of the natural smellscape.

Wilderness Preservation: Protecting Olfactory Heritage for Future Generations:

Wilderness areas, those pristine landscapes that have been relatively untouched by human development, offer a glimpse into the olfactory world as it existed before the advent of industrialization and urbanization. The smellscapes of these areas are often complex and nuanced, reflecting the intricate interplay of plants, animals, and geological processes.

Preserving wilderness areas, therefore, is not just about protecting biodiversity and ecosystem services; it is also about safeguarding olfactory heritage, the unique and irreplaceable scentscapes that have evolved over millennia. These natural smellscapes provide a baseline for understanding the impact of human activities on the olfactory environment and offer a source of inspiration and wonder for future generations.

Wilderness preservation efforts should include a consideration of the olfactory dimension of these landscapes. This can involve monitoring and documenting the smellscapes of wilderness areas, developing management strategies to minimize the impact of human activities on these scentscapes, and promoting olfactory education programs that enhance visitors' appreciation of the natural smellscape.

The Smell of the Wild: Eco-Tourism and the Ethics of Olfactory Consumption:

Eco-tourism, a growing sector of the tourism industry, offers opportunities for individuals to experience and appreciate the natural world, including its unique smellscapes. However, the increasing popularity of eco-tourism also raises ethical questions about the commodification of nature and the potential for human activities to disrupt the very environments we seek to enjoy.

Olfactory consumption, the seeking out of specific smells for pleasure or entertainment, can be a driving force behind eco-tourism. Visitors to national parks, for example, might be drawn to the scent of pine needles in a forest, the salty tang of the ocean, or the sulfurous smell of a geyser. However, the pursuit of these olfactory experiences can lead to increased foot traffic, noise pollution, and other human impacts that can disrupt the delicate balance of these ecosystems.

The ethics of eco-tourism require a careful balancing of the desire to experience and appreciate the natural world with the responsibility to protect and preserve it for future generations. This can involve promoting sustainable tourism practices, such as limiting visitor numbers, encouraging responsible behavior, and investing in conservation efforts to mitigate the impact of human activities on the environment.

The Olfactory Restoration of Damaged Landscapes: Rewilding the Smellscape:

Rewilding, the process of restoring degraded ecosystems to a more natural state, often focuses on reintroducing native plant and animal species to create a more biodiverse and resilient ecosystem. However, rewilding efforts should also consider the olfactory dimension of these landscapes, recognizing the importance of restoring the natural smellscape as part of the overall ecological restoration process.

This can involve planting a diversity of native plant species that release a variety of scents, creating habitats that attract a variety of animal species, and reducing or eliminating sources of anthropogenic odors that can mask or distort natural scents.

The olfactory restoration of damaged landscapes can enhance the aesthetic and ecological value of these environments, creating a more immersive and engaging experience for visitors and restoring the olfactory cues that are essential for the well-being of many animal species.

The Smell of Sustainability: Olfactory Considerations in Environmental Decision-Making:

Olfactory considerations should be integrated into environmental decision-making, recognizing the importance of smell in shaping our perceptions of the environment, influencing our behavior, and contributing to our overall well-being. This can involve:

- **Environmental Impact Assessments:** Including an assessment of the olfactory impacts of proposed projects, such as new industrial facilities, transportation infrastructure, or urban developments.

- **Urban Planning and Design:** Considering the olfactory dimensions of urban spaces, incorporating green spaces, olfactory buffers, and other design elements that promote a healthy and pleasant smellscape.

- **Agricultural Practices:** Promoting sustainable farming practices, such as organic agriculture and agroforestry, that minimize the use of synthetic pesticides and fertilizers, which can release harmful or unpleasant smells into the environment.

- **Waste Management:** Investing in waste management systems that minimize odor emissions and prevent the contamination of air and water with noxious smells.

- **Environmental Education:** Promoting olfactory literacy, the ability to identify, understand, and appreciate a diverse range of smells, as part of broader environmental education programs.

The Future of the Natural Smellscape: Preserving Olfactory Heritage in a Changing World:

The natural smellscape is under increasing pressure from human activities, climate change, and other environmental challenges. Preserving the olfactory heritage of the natural world requires a commitment to conservation, sustainable development, and a deeper understanding of the intricate connections between smell, the environment, and human well-being.

As we move towards a future where smell can be increasingly manipulated and controlled through technology, it is crucial to remember the value of natural scents and the importance of preserving the olfactory richness and diversity of the world around us. This requires embracing a biocentric perspective that recognizes the intrinsic value of all living beings and ecosystems, promoting olfactory equity and environmental justice, and engaging in responsible stewardship of the natural smellscape for the benefit of present and future generations.

Chapter Twenty-Two: Olfactory Education: Cultivating Olfactory Literacy and Promoting Ethical Engagement with the Smellscape

Despite its profound influence on our lives, smell is often the most neglected and misunderstood of our senses. We are taught from a young age to identify colors, shapes, sounds, and textures, but rarely do we receive formal education about the nuances of smell, its cultural significance, or its ethical implications. This chapter explores the importance of olfactory education, examining the benefits of cultivating olfactory literacy, the challenges of incorporating smell into educational curricula, and the potential for olfactory education to foster a deeper appreciation for the world of scent and to promote a more ethical and responsible engagement with the smellscape.

Olfactory Literacy: The Ability to Decode the Language of Smell:

Olfactory literacy, the ability to identify, understand, and appreciate a diverse range of smells, is essential for navigating a world saturated with scents. Just as literacy in language allows us to read, write, and communicate effectively, olfactory literacy empowers us to:

- **Identify and Discriminate Scents:** Olfactory literacy enables us to recognize and distinguish between different smells, expanding our vocabulary of scent and enhancing our ability to appreciate the nuances of the olfactory world. Just as a wine connoisseur can discern the subtle notes of a vintage, an olfactory-literate individual can identify the individual components of a complex fragrance or the subtle shifts in the smellscape of a forest as the seasons change.

- **Understand the Meaning and Context of Smell:**
  Olfactory literacy goes beyond mere identification; it involves understanding the cultural, social, and historical meanings associated with different smells. This includes recognizing how smells are used to communicate information, evoke emotions, and shape our perceptions of the world. For example, an olfactory-literate individual might understand how the smell of incense is used in religious ceremonies, how the aroma of freshly baked bread can create a sense of comfort and hospitality, or how the smell of a particular flower might trigger personal memories or cultural associations.

- **Engage Ethically with the Smellscape:** Olfactory literacy fosters a more ethical and responsible engagement with the smellscape. This includes being mindful of the impact of our own smells on others, respecting the olfactory preferences of those around us, and advocating for a more just and equitable distribution of olfactory resources. For example, an olfactory-literate individual might be more aware of the potential for strong perfumes to trigger allergies or sensitivities in others, more considerate of the smells emanating from their own cooking or pets, and more likely to support policies that address air pollution and promote access to clean air for all.

The Benefits of Olfactory Education: Enhancing Sensory Awareness, Promoting Well-being, and Fostering Environmental Stewardship:

Cultivating olfactory literacy through education can offer a wide range of benefits for individuals, communities, and the environment. Some of the key benefits include:

- **Enhanced Sensory Awareness and Appreciation:**
  Olfactory education can open up a world of sensory experiences, expanding our appreciation for the richness and complexity of the smellscape. Just as learning about music can deepen our enjoyment of a symphony, learning

about smell can enhance our appreciation for the subtle nuances of a fragrance, the evolving smellscape of a garden, or the evocative scents of a bustling city street.

- **Improved Physical and Mental Health:** Smell is intimately linked to our physical and mental well-being. Certain scents can have a calming or stimulating effect, reducing stress, improving mood, and even enhancing cognitive function. Olfactory education can empower individuals to use scent to promote their own well-being, whether it's using essential oils for relaxation, incorporating fragrant plants into their homes, or simply being more mindful of the positive and negative impacts of different smells on their mood and health.

- **Enhanced Safety and Risk Awareness:** Smell plays a crucial role in alerting us to potential dangers, such as smoke, gas leaks, or spoiled food. Olfactory education can improve our ability to recognize and respond to these olfactory warning signals, potentially preventing accidents or injuries.

- **Deeper Understanding of Culture and History:** Smell is deeply embedded in cultural practices and historical traditions. Olfactory education can provide insights into the role of smell in different cultures, from the use of incense in religious ceremonies to the significance of certain scents in traditional cuisines. This understanding can foster greater cultural appreciation and sensitivity.

- **Increased Empathy and Compassion:** Olfactory education can foster empathy and compassion for individuals with olfactory disabilities, such as anosmia or hyposmia. By understanding the challenges they face, we can become more aware of the importance of olfactory inclusivity and more sensitive to the needs of those who navigate life without a functional sense of smell.

- **Enhanced Environmental Awareness and Stewardship:** Olfactory education can foster a deeper appreciation for the natural smellscape and the importance of preserving olfactory heritage. By understanding the role of smell in ecological processes and the impact of human activities on the olfactory environment, individuals can become more responsible stewards of the natural world.

Integrating Smell into Education: Challenges and Opportunities in Curriculum Development:

Incorporating smell into educational curricula presents unique challenges, as smell is often considered a less "academic" sense compared to sight or hearing. However, with careful planning and creative approaches, smell can be integrated into a wide range of subjects, enriching learning experiences and fostering olfactory literacy.

Some of the challenges and opportunities in integrating smell into education include:

- **The Subjectivity of Smell:** The perception of smell is highly subjective, influenced by individual differences in olfactory sensitivity, cultural backgrounds, and personal experiences. This subjectivity presents a challenge for educators, who must be mindful of the diverse olfactory perceptions of their students and avoid imposing their own olfactory preferences or biases. However, the subjectivity of smell can also be an opportunity for engaging students in discussions about sensory diversity, cultural differences, and the role of personal experience in shaping our perceptions of the world.

- **The Ephemeral Nature of Smell:** Smell is a fleeting and transient sense, making it challenging to capture and preserve olfactory experiences in a traditional classroom setting. However, educators can use a variety of techniques to overcome this challenge, such as using essential oils, natural materials, or even commercially available scent diffusers to create specific olfactory experiences for students.

- **The Safety of Olfactory Materials:** Some scents can trigger allergic reactions or sensitivities in certain individuals. Educators must be mindful of these potential risks and take steps to ensure the safety of their students, such as providing clear warnings about the use of potentially allergenic ingredients, offering alternative scent-free experiences, and having a plan in place to address potential allergic reactions.

- **The Cultural Sensitivity of Smell:** Smell is deeply embedded in cultural practices and traditions, and educators must be sensitive to the cultural meanings and associations of different smells. This includes avoiding the use of scents that might be considered offensive or inappropriate in certain cultures and being mindful of the diverse olfactory experiences of students from different backgrounds.

Despite these challenges, there are many opportunities for integrating smell into education in a meaningful and engaging way. Some examples include:

- **Science Education:** Smell can be incorporated into science lessons about the human olfactory system, the chemistry of odorants, the role of smell in animal behavior, or the impact of human activities on the olfactory environment. Students can engage in hands-on activities, such as creating their own fragrances, conducting olfactory experiments, or analyzing the smellscapes of different environments.

- **History and Social Studies Education:** Smell can be used to bring history to life, recreating the smellscapes of different historical periods or using scent to evoke the sensory experiences of past events. For example, students might learn about the role of incense in ancient Egyptian rituals, the smells of the battlefield during the Civil War, or the olfactory impact of industrialization on urban environments.

- **Literature and Language Arts Education:** Smell is often used in literature to create atmosphere, evoke emotions, and develop characters. Students can explore the use of olfactory imagery in poetry, novels, and plays, analyzing how authors use scent to enhance their storytelling.

- **Art Education:** Smell can be incorporated into art lessons, exploring the use of scent as an artistic medium, creating olfactory installations, or analyzing the olfactory dimensions of traditional art forms.

- **Culinary Arts Education:** Smell is essential for the enjoyment and appreciation of food. Students can learn about the role of smell in flavor perception, the cultural significance of different scents in cuisine, and the ethics of food production and consumption from an olfactory perspective.

- **Environmental Education:** Smell can be used to enhance environmental awareness and stewardship, exploring the importance of preserving natural scents, the impact of human activities on the olfactory environment, and the ethical considerations of olfactory consumption in eco-tourism.

Olfactory Education for All Ages: Engaging the Senses from Early Childhood to Adulthood:

Olfactory education can be tailored to different age groups and learning styles, engaging the senses and fostering olfactory literacy from early childhood to adulthood.

- **Early Childhood Education:** Young children are naturally curious about the world of smell, and olfactory education can foster their sensory exploration and development. Simple activities, such as smelling different fruits, flowers, or spices, can introduce children to the diversity of scents and help them to develop their olfactory vocabulary. Storybooks that incorporate olfactory elements, such as scratch-and-sniff books, can also engage young children's senses and stimulate their imaginations.

- **Elementary and Middle School Education:** Olfactory education can be integrated into a variety of subjects, such as science, history, language arts, and art. Hands-on activities, such as creating fragrance blends, conducting olfactory experiments, or analyzing the smellscapes of different environments, can engage students' senses and make learning more interactive and memorable.

- **High School Education:** Students can explore more complex olfactory concepts, such as the chemistry of odorants, the psychology of smell, the ethics of olfactory technology, and the role of smell in culture and society. They can also engage in research projects, such as investigating the impact of air pollution on the olfactory environment or designing olfactory-inclusive spaces.

- **Higher Education:** Olfactory studies are emerging as a field of academic inquiry, with universities offering courses and degree programs in areas such as sensory science, perfumery, olfactory art, and the ethics of smell. These programs provide students with a deeper understanding of the science, culture, and ethics of olfaction.

- **Adult Education:** Olfactory education can be a lifelong pursuit, with opportunities for adults to learn about smell through workshops, lectures, museum exhibits, and even online courses. These programs can enhance sensory awareness, promote well-being, and foster a deeper appreciation for the world of scent.

Olfactory Education as a Catalyst for Social Change: Promoting Olfactory Justice, Environmental Stewardship, and a More Inclusive Smellscape:

Olfactory education has the potential to be a catalyst for social change, promoting a more just, equitable, and sustainable relationship with the smellscape.

By fostering olfactory literacy, we can empower individuals to make more informed decisions about their own olfactory experiences, to advocate for a more inclusive and accessible olfactory environment, and to become more responsible stewards of the natural smellscape.

Olfactory education can also play a role in addressing environmental injustices, promoting olfactory equity, and raising awareness of the impact of human activities on the olfactory environment.

By cultivating a deeper understanding and appreciation for the world of smell, olfactory education can pave the way for a more fragrant and just future for all.

Chapter Twenty-Three: The Ethics of Olfactory Research: Informed Consent, Sensory Experimentation, and the Moral Responsibilities of Olfactory Scientists

The human sense of smell, once shrouded in mystery, is gradually yielding its secrets to scientific inquiry. Advances in neuroscience, genetics, and psychology are providing a deeper understanding of the intricate workings of the olfactory system, its role in our emotions and behaviors, and its impact on our health and well-being. This burgeoning field of olfactory research holds immense promise for developing new therapies for olfactory disorders, creating innovative technologies that enhance our olfactory experiences, and deepening our understanding of the human condition. However, as with any scientific endeavor that probes the complexities of human perception and experience, olfactory research raises a unique set of ethical considerations that must be carefully navigated to ensure the responsible and ethical conduct of research. This chapter explores the ethical challenges and responsibilities inherent in olfactory research, examining the importance of informed consent, the unique vulnerabilities of sensory experimentation, and the obligation of olfactory scientists to conduct their research with integrity, transparency, and a commitment to the well-being of their subjects and society as a whole.

Informed Consent: Respecting the Autonomy of Olfactory Research Participants:

The cornerstone of ethical research, regardless of the field of inquiry, is the principle of informed consent. This principle recognizes the right of individuals to make autonomous decisions about their participation in research, based on a clear understanding of the risks and benefits involved. In the context of olfactory research, obtaining informed consent presents unique challenges, as the nature of olfactory experiences, the potential for emotional and psychological responses to smells, and the evolving understanding of the long-term effects of olfactory stimulation require careful consideration and clear communication to ensure that participants are fully informed and empowered to make their own decisions about participation.

One of the key challenges in obtaining informed consent for olfactory research is the difficulty of accurately conveying the nature of the olfactory experience to potential participants. Unlike visual or auditory stimuli, which can be easily described or demonstrated, smells are subjective and ephemeral, making it challenging to articulate the precise qualities of a scent or the potential range of emotional and psychological responses it might evoke. Researchers must find creative ways to communicate the nature of the olfactory stimuli that will be used in the research, using vivid descriptions, analogies to familiar smells, or even pre-testing scents with a small group of volunteers to gauge the range of potential reactions.

The potential for emotional and psychological responses to smells also requires careful consideration in the informed consent process. Certain scents can trigger strong memories, emotions, or even physical sensations, particularly for individuals with a history of trauma or olfactory sensitivities. Researchers must be aware of these potential risks and screen participants carefully to identify those who might be vulnerable to adverse reactions. The informed consent process should clearly outline these potential risks, providing participants with the opportunity to ask questions and to withdraw from the research at any time if they feel uncomfortable or distressed.

The evolving understanding of the long-term effects of olfactory stimulation also requires ongoing evaluation and transparency in the informed consent process. As research progresses, new insights into the potential impacts of olfactory stimulation on brain function, behavior, and even health may emerge. Researchers have an ethical obligation to stay informed about these developments and to update their informed consent procedures accordingly, ensuring that participants are aware of the latest findings and any potential long-term risks associated with their participation.

Sensory Experimentation: Navigating the Unique Vulnerabilities of Olfactory Research:

Olfactory research often involves exposing participants to a variety of smells, some of which may be unpleasant, unfamiliar, or even potentially triggering for certain individuals. This sensory experimentation raises ethical concerns about the potential for psychological harm, the importance of minimizing discomfort, and the need for careful monitoring of participants' well-being throughout the research process.

One of the key ethical challenges in olfactory research is the potential for psychological harm. Exposure to certain smells can trigger negative emotions, such as disgust, fear, or anxiety, particularly for individuals with a history of trauma or olfactory sensitivities. Researchers must be mindful of these potential risks and take steps to mitigate them, such as carefully screening participants, using scents that are generally considered to be safe and non-toxic, and providing participants with the opportunity to opt out of any part of the research that they find uncomfortable or distressing.

Minimizing discomfort is also an important ethical consideration in olfactory research. Even scents that are not inherently unpleasant can become overwhelming or irritating if presented at high concentrations or for extended periods of time. Researchers should strive to use the lowest concentration of scent necessary to achieve the research objectives and to limit the duration of exposure to minimize any potential discomfort for participants.

Careful monitoring of participants' well-being throughout the research process is essential to ensure their safety and comfort. Researchers should observe participants for any signs of distress or discomfort, such as changes in facial expression, body language, or verbal reports. They should also provide participants with the opportunity to ask questions, express concerns, or withdraw from the research at any time.

The Moral Responsibilities of Olfactory Scientists: Integrity, Transparency, and Public Trust:

Olfactory scientists, like all researchers, have a moral responsibility to conduct their research with integrity, transparency, and a commitment to the well-being of their subjects and society as a whole. This responsibility extends beyond the immediate context of the research study, encompassing the dissemination of research findings, the potential applications of olfactory technology, and the broader social and ethical implications of their work.

Integrity in olfactory research involves adhering to the highest ethical standards in all aspects of the research process, from the design and execution of the study to the analysis and reporting of the findings. This includes ensuring the accuracy and objectivity of data collection and analysis, avoiding bias in the interpretation of results, and disclosing any potential conflicts of interest that might influence the research.

Transparency is crucial for maintaining public trust in olfactory research. Researchers should be open and transparent about their research methods, data collection procedures, and any potential risks or benefits associated with the research. They should also be willing to share their findings with the public, both through peer-reviewed publications and through public outreach and education initiatives.

Olfactory scientists also have a responsibility to consider the potential applications of their research and the broader social and ethical implications of their work. The development of new olfactory technologies, such as electronic noses, olfactory displays, and olfactory implants, raises a host of ethical questions about privacy, surveillance, manipulation, and the potential for these technologies to be used for harmful or exploitative purposes. Olfactory scientists have a responsibility to engage in open and honest dialogue with the public about these issues, to advocate for the responsible use of olfactory technologies, and to work towards ensuring that these technologies are used for the benefit of society as a whole.

Ethical Review and Oversight: Ensuring the Responsible Conduct of Olfactory Research:

To ensure the ethical conduct of olfactory research, independent review and oversight are essential. Institutional Review Boards (IRBs), which are committees charged with reviewing and approving research involving human subjects, play a crucial role in evaluating the ethical implications of olfactory research, ensuring that the rights and well-being of participants are protected.

IRBs review research proposals to assess the potential risks and benefits of the research, the adequacy of informed consent procedures, the procedures for minimizing discomfort and protecting participant privacy, and the overall ethical soundness of the research design. They also monitor ongoing research studies to ensure that they are being conducted ethically and that any unexpected or adverse events are reported and addressed promptly.

The involvement of IRBs in the review and oversight of olfactory research helps to ensure that research is conducted ethically and responsibly, minimizing the potential for harm to participants and maximizing the potential benefits of research for society as a whole.

Emerging Ethical Challenges in Olfactory Research:

As olfactory research continues to advance, new ethical challenges are emerging that require careful consideration and ongoing dialogue between scientists, ethicists, policymakers, and the public.

Some of the emerging ethical challenges in olfactory research include:

- **The Use of Olfactory Data in Artificial Intelligence (AI):** The increasing availability of olfactory data is opening up new possibilities for using this data in AI applications, such as developing algorithms that can predict consumer preferences, diagnose diseases, or even identify individuals based on their unique olfactory profile. The use of olfactory data in AI raises ethical concerns about privacy, surveillance, and the potential for algorithmic bias.

- **The Ethical Implications of Olfactory Enhancement Technologies:** The development of technologies that can enhance or restore the sense of smell, such as electronic noses and olfactory implants, raises ethical questions about accessibility, equity, and the potential for these technologies to be used to manipulate or control individuals' olfactory experiences.

- **The Olfactory Dimension of Virtual Reality (VR) and Augmented Reality (AR):** The integration of olfactory displays into VR and AR environments creates new possibilities for immersive and interactive olfactory experiences, but also raises ethical questions about the potential for these technologies to be used for manipulative or exploitative purposes, such as triggering specific emotions or memories or creating a sense of dependence on virtual olfactory experiences.

- **The Olfactory Impacts of Climate Change:** Climate change is altering the smellscapes of the world around us, with rising temperatures, changing precipitation patterns, and increasing air pollution affecting the scents of plants, animals, and even the air we breathe. The olfactory dimensions of climate change raise ethical questions about the loss of olfactory heritage, the potential for olfactory disruptions to affect human health and well-being, and the need for climate adaptation strategies that consider the olfactory environment.

Olfactory Ethics and the Future of Smell Research:

The field of olfactory research is poised for continued growth and innovation, offering the potential to deepen our understanding of the human sense of smell, develop new therapies for olfactory disorders, and create innovative technologies that enhance our olfactory experiences. However, as we explore this fascinating and complex sensory world, it is crucial that we do so with a strong ethical compass, ensuring that research is conducted responsibly, that the rights and well-being of participants are protected, and that the potential benefits of olfactory research are shared equitably and ethically with society as a whole.

The development of a robust framework for olfactory ethics, grounded in principles of respect, autonomy, beneficence, and justice, is essential for guiding olfactory research and ensuring its responsible and ethical conduct. This framework should address the unique vulnerabilities of sensory experimentation, the importance of informed consent, the challenges of protecting olfactory data, and the broader social and ethical implications of olfactory technology.

The future of smell research depends on the commitment of olfactory scientists to ethical principles and practices. By embracing transparency, engaging in open dialogue with the public, and prioritizing the well-being of both human and non-human participants, olfactory research can continue to unlock the secrets of our sense of smell, enriching our understanding of the world and our place within it.

Chapter Twenty-Four: Olfactory Justice: Legal Frameworks, Environmental Regulations, and the Pursuit of Olfactory Equity

The air we breathe, often taken for granted, is a shared resource, a commons that transcends individual boundaries and connects us to our environment and to each other. The quality of this shared air, including its olfactory dimensions, is not simply a matter of personal preference or aesthetic sensibility; it is a matter of social justice, with profound implications for public health, environmental equity, and the well-being of communities. This chapter explores the legal frameworks and environmental regulations that have emerged to address olfactory nuisances, air pollution, and the pursuit of olfactory justice, examining the challenges of regulating smells, the evolving legal standards for olfactory harms, and the role of community activism in shaping a more equitable and fragrant world.

The Challenge of Regulating Smells: Objectivity vs. Subjectivity in Olfactory Law:

The legal regulation of smells presents unique challenges, as the perception of smell is inherently subjective, influenced by individual sensitivities, cultural backgrounds, and personal experiences. What one person finds offensive or unbearable, another may find tolerable or even pleasant. This subjectivity makes it difficult to establish objective legal standards for what constitutes an olfactory nuisance or to quantify the harm caused by unpleasant smells.

Traditional nuisance laws, rooted in common law principles, have often struggled to address olfactory nuisances effectively. These laws typically require a plaintiff to demonstrate that the smell in question constitutes an "unreasonable interference" with the use and enjoyment of their property. However, the determination of what constitutes an "unreasonable interference" is often left to the discretion of judges and juries, leading to inconsistent rulings and a lack of clear legal precedents.

The quantification of harm caused by olfactory nuisances is another challenge in olfactory law. Unlike other environmental harms, such as noise pollution or water contamination, which can be measured and quantified using objective metrics, the harm caused by unpleasant smells is often difficult to assess. While some studies have attempted to quantify the economic impacts of olfactory nuisances, such as decreased property values or reduced tourism revenue, the psychological and emotional impacts of unpleasant smells are often difficult to measure and are not always reflected in traditional legal remedies.

Environmental Regulations and Air Quality Standards: Addressing Olfactory Pollution as a Public Health Concern:

Recognizing the public health implications of air pollution, including its olfactory dimensions, governments have enacted a variety of environmental regulations and air quality standards aimed at mitigating the release of harmful or unpleasant smells into the atmosphere. These regulations often target specific sources of olfactory pollution, such as industrial facilities, waste management sites, and agricultural operations, establishing emission limits, requiring the implementation of odor control technologies, and imposing penalties for violations.

The Clean Air Act (CAA) in the United States, for example, is a comprehensive federal law that regulates air pollution from both stationary and mobile sources. The CAA authorizes the Environmental Protection Agency (EPA) to set National Ambient Air Quality Standards (NAAQS) for six common air pollutants, including ozone, particulate matter, carbon monoxide, sulfur dioxide, nitrogen dioxide, and lead. While the CAA does not explicitly address odor pollution, the EPA has the authority to regulate odors under the "general nuisance" provision of the act, which prohibits the emission of air pollutants that "may reasonably be anticipated to endanger public health or welfare."

The EPA has also developed guidance documents for addressing odor pollution, recommending best practices for odor control and encouraging states and local governments to develop their own odor regulations. Many states and local jurisdictions have enacted their own odor ordinances, often using a combination of objective and subjective standards to define and regulate olfactory nuisances.

Objective standards, such as odor concentration limits or odor emission rates, attempt to quantify the amount of odor-causing compounds released into the atmosphere. These standards are often based on scientific measurements and can be enforced using air monitoring equipment. Subjective standards, such as odor intensity scales or community odor surveys, rely on human perception to assess the offensiveness or impact of smells. These standards can be more challenging to enforce, as they rely on subjective judgments and can be influenced by individual sensitivities and cultural backgrounds.

The Pursuit of Olfactory Justice: Community Activism and the Fight for a More Equitable Smellscape:

The pursuit of olfactory justice often involves grassroots activism and community organizing, as marginalized communities that are disproportionately burdened by olfactory nuisances and air pollution fight for a more equitable and healthy smellscape. These communities often face systemic barriers to environmental justice, including a lack of political power, limited access to legal resources, and the perception that their olfactory concerns are not taken seriously by government agencies or industry representatives.

Community activists have employed a variety of strategies to address olfactory injustices, including:

- **Community Odor Monitoring:** Organizing community members to monitor and document odor pollution in their neighborhoods, using citizen science tools and techniques to gather data on the frequency, intensity, and location of unpleasant smells.

- **Public Awareness Campaigns:** Raising awareness of olfactory pollution and its impacts on public health and quality of life through community meetings, public forums, media outreach, and social media campaigns.

- **Advocacy for Stronger Regulations:** Pressuring government agencies to enact and enforce stricter odor regulations, holding public officials accountable for addressing olfactory nuisances, and advocating for greater transparency and community participation in environmental decision-making processes.

- **Legal Action:** Filing lawsuits against polluting industries or government agencies that fail to address olfactory nuisances, seeking injunctive relief to stop or reduce odor emissions and seeking compensation for damages caused by olfactory pollution.

- **Community-Based Solutions:** Developing and implementing community-based solutions to mitigate odor pollution, such as planting trees and other vegetation to create olfactory buffers, promoting the use of natural odor control methods, and advocating for the relocation of polluting industries away from residential areas.

The success of these community-led efforts often depends on the ability to build coalitions with other environmental justice groups, to mobilize public support, and to hold those in power accountable for addressing olfactory injustices.

Case Studies in Olfactory Justice: From "Cancer Alley" to Hog Farm Communities:

The fight for olfactory justice has played out in communities across the United States and around the world, as marginalized communities have challenged the unequal distribution of olfactory burdens and demanded a more equitable and healthy smellscape.

One of the most well-known examples of olfactory justice activism is the case of "Cancer Alley," an 85-mile stretch of land along the Mississippi River between Baton Rouge and New Orleans, Louisiana. This area is home to a high concentration of petrochemical plants and refineries, and it has some of the highest cancer rates in the country. The residents of Cancer Alley, many of whom are African American, have long complained about the noxious smells emanating from these industrial facilities, which they believe are contributing to the high rates of cancer and other health problems in the region.

Community activists in Cancer Alley have organized protests, filed lawsuits, and lobbied government agencies to address the environmental injustices they face, including the olfactory burden of industrial pollution. Their efforts have led to increased scrutiny of the petrochemical industry, stricter environmental regulations, and some progress in reducing air pollution and odor emissions in the region.

Another example of olfactory justice activism can be found in communities that are located near large-scale hog farms, also known as Concentrated Animal Feeding Operations (CAFOs). CAFOs produce vast quantities of manure and other waste products that release strong and pervasive odors into the surrounding environment. These odors can travel for miles, affecting the quality of life of nearby residents, causing respiratory problems, headaches, nausea, and stress.

Hog farms are disproportionately located in or near communities of color and low-income communities, reflecting a history of racial discrimination and economic inequality in the agricultural industry. Residents of these communities have organized to challenge the siting of hog farms in their neighborhoods, demanding stricter regulations on odor emissions, greater transparency in permitting processes, and compensation for damages caused by olfactory pollution.

These case studies highlight the challenges and complexities of pursuing olfactory justice, the importance of community activism in holding those in power accountable, and the potential for legal frameworks and environmental regulations to play a role in creating a more equitable and fragrant world.

The Evolving Legal Landscape of Olfactory Justice: New Frontiers in Environmental Law:

The legal landscape of olfactory justice is constantly evolving as courts, legislatures, and regulatory agencies grapple with the challenges of regulating smells, quantifying olfactory harms, and balancing competing interests in the smellscape. New legal theories and approaches are emerging to address the unique challenges of olfactory pollution and to provide more effective remedies for communities that are disproportionately burdened by unpleasant smells.

One emerging legal theory is the concept of "olfactory property rights," which recognizes that individuals have a right to enjoy their property free from unreasonable olfactory interference. This theory could provide a basis for legal action against polluting industries or individuals who create olfactory nuisances that diminish the value or enjoyment of neighboring properties.

Another emerging legal approach is the use of "hedonic damages" in olfactory nuisance cases. Hedonic damages are a type of compensation for the loss of enjoyment of life, often used in cases where the harm suffered is difficult to quantify in monetary terms. In the context of olfactory nuisances, hedonic damages could be awarded to compensate individuals for the diminished quality of life caused by exposure to unpleasant smells.

The development of new technologies for measuring and monitoring odors is also shaping the legal landscape of olfactory justice. Electronic noses and other olfactory sensors can provide more objective and quantifiable data on odor pollution, strengthening the evidence base for legal action and facilitating the enforcement of odor regulations.

The pursuit of olfactory justice is an ongoing struggle, as communities continue to fight for a more equitable and fragrant world. The evolving legal landscape, with its emerging theories, approaches, and technologies, offers new tools and strategies for addressing olfactory injustices and ensuring that all individuals have the right to breathe clean air and enjoy a pleasant smellscape.

The Right to a Fragrant Future: Towards a More Just and Equitable Olfactory World:

The pursuit of olfactory justice is not just about mitigating unpleasant smells or punishing polluters; it is about creating a more just and equitable world where all individuals have the right to breathe clean air, enjoy a pleasant smellscape, and experience the full range of olfactory experiences that enrich our lives.

This requires a fundamental shift in our understanding of smell, recognizing its importance not only for our sensory pleasure but also for our health, well-being, and our connection to the natural world. It also requires a commitment to environmental justice, ensuring that the benefits and burdens of the smellscape are distributed equitably across all communities.

The legal frameworks and environmental regulations discussed in this chapter are essential tools for achieving olfactory justice. However, they are not sufficient on their own. A truly just and equitable olfactory world requires a collective effort from individuals, communities, industry, and government, working together to create a more fragrant and harmonious future for all.

Chapter Twenty-Five: Towards an Olfactory Ethos: Rethinking Our Relationship with Smell in a World of Sensory Overload

We live in a world awash in sensory stimuli, bombarded by sights, sounds, and information competing for our attention. In this cacophony of sensory input, our sense of smell, often relegated to the background of our conscious awareness, can easily be overwhelmed or ignored. Yet, as we have explored throughout this book, smell plays a far more profound role in shaping our experiences, emotions, and relationships than we might realize. It influences our perceptions of the world, shapes our identities, and guides our interactions with others, often operating beneath the level of conscious awareness, subtly shaping our thoughts, feelings, and behaviors.

As we move towards a future where smell can be increasingly manipulated, controlled, and even synthetically generated through technology, the need for a thoughtful and nuanced olfactory ethos, a set of ethical principles and values that guide our relationship with smell, becomes increasingly urgent. This olfactory ethos must acknowledge the power of smell, its potential for both good and harm, and the responsibility we have to use our olfactory senses ethically and responsibly in a world where the boundaries between the natural and the synthetic, the real and the virtual, are becoming increasingly blurred.

A key element of this olfactory ethos is the recognition that smell is not merely a personal preference or a matter of individual taste; it is a shared sense, a common language that connects us to each other and to the world around us. The smells we create, whether intentionally or unintentionally, can have an impact on others, triggering memories, emotions, and even physical reactions. This recognition of the interconnectedness of our olfactory experiences calls for a sense of olfactory empathy, a willingness to consider the impact of our smells on others and to strive to create a harmonious and equitable olfactory environment for all.

Olfactory empathy extends beyond our immediate human interactions to encompass our relationship with the natural world. The smellscapes of forests, oceans, and meadows are not merely pleasant backdrops for our sensory enjoyment; they are integral parts of the ecosystems that support life on Earth. The scents released by plants, animals, and even the soil play crucial roles in ecological processes, from pollination and seed dispersal to nutrient cycling and decomposition.

As we navigate an increasingly synthetic olfactory world, where technology allows us to create any smell imaginable, it is essential to remember the value of natural scents and the importance of preserving the olfactory richness and diversity of the planet. This requires a commitment to environmental stewardship, a recognition of the intrinsic value of natural smellscapes, and a willingness to minimize our olfactory impact on the environment.

The pursuit of olfactory justice, a central theme throughout this book, must also be a guiding principle of our olfactory ethos. Olfactory justice recognizes the unequal distribution of olfactory burdens and benefits in our society, the disproportionate exposure of marginalized communities to noxious smells and air pollution, and the need for a more equitable and fragrant world for all. This requires challenging the olfactory hierarchies that privilege certain smells while stigmatizing others, addressing the root causes of olfactory inequality, and ensuring that all individuals have the right to breathe clean air, enjoy a pleasant smellscape, and experience the full range of olfactory experiences that enrich our lives.

Olfactory literacy, the ability to identify, understand, and appreciate a diverse range of smells, is essential for cultivating a more nuanced and ethical relationship with smell. Just as literacy in language empowers us to communicate effectively and to navigate the complexities of human interaction, olfactory literacy empowers us to decode the language of scent, to understand its cultural and social meanings, and to engage with the smellscape in a more informed and responsible way. Olfactory education, encompassing a wide range of formal and informal learning experiences, can play a crucial role in fostering olfactory literacy, from introducing young children to the diversity of scents to engaging adults in discussions about the ethics of olfactory technology and the social justice implications of smell.

The future of smell is full of possibilities, both exciting and daunting. The ability to capture, recreate, and even enhance the sense of smell through technology has the potential to revolutionize a wide range of fields, from healthcare and entertainment to environmental monitoring and urban planning. However, these technological advancements also raise profound ethical questions about authenticity, privacy, manipulation, and the potential for unintended consequences. As we explore this uncharted olfactory territory, it is crucial that we do so with a strong ethical compass, guided by the principles of olfactory empathy, justice, literacy, and environmental stewardship.

The development of a robust olfactory ethos, a shared understanding of the ethical dimensions of smell, is essential for navigating the challenges and opportunities of this emerging olfactory era. This ethos must be grounded in a deep appreciation for the power of smell, its potential for both good and harm, and the responsibility we have to use our olfactory senses wisely and ethically in a world where smell is becoming an increasingly potent force.

Printed in Great Britain
by Amazon